The Country Seats of the United States

PENN STUDIES IN LANDSCAPE ARCHITECTURE

John Dixon Hunt, Series Editor

This series is dedicated to the study and promotion of a wide variety of approaches to landscape architecture, with special emphasis on connections between theory and practice. It includes monographs on key topics in history and theory, descriptions of projects by both established and rising designers, translations of major foreign-language texts, anthologies of theoretical and historical writings on classic issues, and critical writing by members of the profession of landscape architecture. The series was the recipient of the Award of Honor in Communications from the American Society of Landscape Architects, 2006.

The Country Seats of the United States

William Russell Birch

Edited with an Introduction by
Emily T. Cooperman

UNIVERSITY OF PENNSYLVANIA PRESS
PHILADELPHIA

Published with the assistance of the Getty Foundation.

Copyright © 2009 University of Pennsylvania Press

All rights reserved. Except for brief quotations used for purposes of review or scholarly citation, none of this book may be reproduced in any form by any means without written permission from the publisher.

Published by
University of Pennsylvania Press
Philadelphia, Pennsylvania 19104-4112

Printed in Canada on acid-free paper
10 9 8 7 6 5 4 3 2 1

LIBRARY OF CONGRESS CATALOGING-IN-PUBLICATION DATA

Birch, William Russell, 1755–1834.
  The country seats of the United States / William Russell Birch ; edited with an introduction by Emily T. Cooperman.
    "First issued ... in 1808"—Introduction.
    p. cm. (Penn studies in landscape architecture)
    Includes bibliographical references and index.
    ISBN 978-0-8122-4132-7 (alk. paper)
    1. Historic buildings—United States. 2. Historic buildings—United States—Pictorial works. 3. Landscape architecture—United States—History—19th century. 4. Suburban homes—United States—History—19th century. 5. Historic buildings—Middle Atlantic States. 6. Historic buildings—Pennsylvania. 7. United States—Description and travel. 8. United States—History, Local. 9. Middle Atlantic States—History, Local. 10. Pennsylvania—History, Local. I. Cooperman, Emily T.
E164 .B61 2009
973.22   2008022364

CONTENTS

vii LOCATIONS OF COUNTRY SEATS

1 INTRODUCTION

3 Artistic Formation in Britain
8 Les Délices de la Grande Bretagne
12 The Philadelphia Scene and Early Success in America
15 Landscape Designs and Picturesque Tours
21 Country Seats
30 Suburban Villas

39 THE COUNTRY SEATS OF THE UNITED STATES

46 Hoboken
HOBOKEN, NEW JERSEY

48 Hampton
TOWSON, MARYLAND

50 Lansdowne
PHILADELPHIA, PENNSYLVANIA

52 Echo
PHILADELPHIA, PENNSYLVANIA

54 Mount Vernon
ALEXANDRIA, VIRGINIA

56 Fountain Green
PHILADELPHIA, PENNSYLVANIA

58 Solitude
PHILADELPHIA, PENNSYLVANIA

60 Devon
BUCKS COUNTY, PENNSYLVANIA

62 Mount Sidney
PHILADELPHIA, PENNSYLVANIA

64 The Seat of Mr. Duplantier (Delord-Sarpy Mansion)
NEW ORLEANS, LOUISIANA

66 Montebello
BALTIMORE, MARYLAND

68 Woodlands
PHILADELPHIA, PENNSYLVANIA

70 Sedgeley
PHILADELPHIA, PENNSYLVANIA

72 Belmont
PHILADELPHIA, PENNSYLVANIA

74 York Island
NEW YORK, NEW YORK

76 Mendenhall Ferry
PHILADELPHIA, PENNSYLVANIA

78 China Retreat
BUCKS COUNTY, PENNSYLVANIA

80 Springland
BUCKS COUNTY, PENNSYLVANIA

83 INDEX

87 ACKNOWLEDGMENTS

LOCATIONS OF COUNTRY SEATS

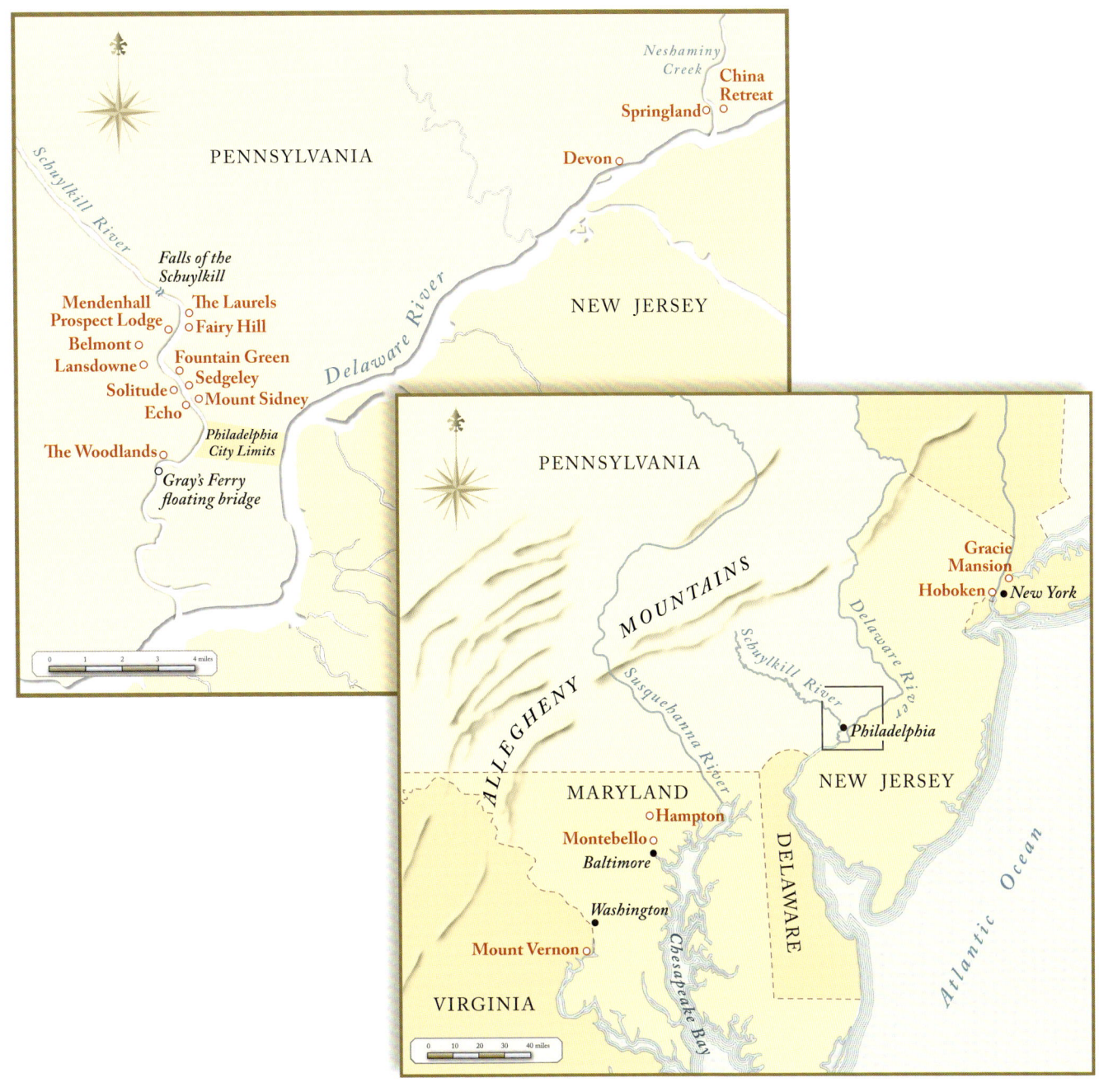

INTRODUCTION

The *Country Seats of the United States of North America*, first issued by William Russell Birch (1755–1834) in 1808, was the second set of engraved views to be published anywhere in the United States, after his *City of Philadelphia in the State of Pennsylvania, North America, as it Appeared in the Year 1800*. No other similar set would be published until Joshua Shaw's *Picturesque Views of American Scenery* appeared in 1820. Although the *Country Seats* did not garner the level of popular support its author had hoped for, the central themes of the book—the emphasis on the suburban house and garden and an appreciation of American nature—were prescient, as they remain crucial topics in the understanding, use, shaping, and consumption of the American landscape to the present. British eighteenth-century publications of country houses showed the estates of landed gentry and aristocracy throughout the countryside as well as near London. In contrast, Birch restricted his subjects to houses in the geographic range of the greatest concentration of American cities in the period—between New York and Washington, D.C. (with the exception of one house in New Orleans included to represent the Louisiana Purchase)—although estates in more rural situations were certainly known to him. He thus emphasized the suburban home in what was then the commercial and political heart of the new country.

The preoccupation with country residence and garden remain one of the strongest forces in American culture to the present. The suburb remains alive and well, and has even, it might be argued, mutated to give rise to the contemporary "exurb." Fundamentally, however, the obsession with country (as the obverse of urban) life survives. Birch's opening point of the introduction of the *Country Seats* is that socially and artistically cultivated suburban life would play a key role in the formation of an American civilization. This theme would not become popular until later in the nineteenth century: it appears, for example, twenty-five years after Birch's publication in Andrew Jackson Downing's more successful works. Downing's preface to his *Architecture of Country Houses* (1850) and Birch's for the *Country Seats* have some striking points in common along these lines, including Downing's statement that "it is the solitude and freedom of the family home in the country which constantly preserves the purity of the nation, and invigorates the intellectual powers."[1]

Equally important in connection with later developments in American landscape art (both graphic representation and interventions on the ground) as well as Americans' understanding of their native land was Birch's emphasis on the aesthetics of the picturesque and an ability to value "wild unregulated" nature. The appreciation for and conservation of natural areas conceived of as both aesthetically appealing and untouched by human activity is a commonplace in American culture today, but at the time of the *Country Seats* this visual (and verbal), indeed rhetorical, understanding of wild terrain was not universally held.[2]

The *Country Seats* is also significant as a record, both of the places depicted and of Birch's own work as a landscape designer. The *Country Seats*, in a manner that is complementary to the *City of Philadelphia* (which showed the "eminence of an opulent city" to an unprecedented degree), provides important and sometimes sole documentation of these properties, although neither publication should be reduced to the simple recording of visual fact.[3] Of those residences shown in the nineteen views of the original edition of the *Country Seats* that survive to the present (Hampton, Mount Vernon, Solitude, the Woodlands, Belmont, and Gracie

Mansion), virtually all have been recognized for their design and/or their historical significance, and most are public sites.[4] In addition, the *Country Seats* records not just individual "rural residences" but the suburban villa districts that existed in the areas surrounding important metropolitan centers in the United States in the late eighteenth and early nineteenth century. For example, a number of the villas along the Schuylkill River survive in Philadelphia to this day in the city's Fairmount Park, but the close geographic relationship between city and suburb, and between the worlds of *negotium* and *otium* in the early American republic, is nowhere better represented than in the *Country Seats*.

Finally, the *Country Seats* is a record of Birch's landscape designs at his own property, Springland, and of the aesthetic that informed both his graphic views and designs. It also indicates the activities of a generation of artists and practitioners who have largely either disappeared from view or been overshadowed by later figures.[5] Birch was among a group of designers and painters who emigrated to the young United States from Britain during the last decade of the eighteenth century, expecting to find a ready market for the native landscape views like those that had become popular in England, and also to find their place in the society of the new nation as professionals rather than craftsmen or tradesmen. For the most part, they, like Birch, were disappointed in the response to these two key expectations. It would take two more generations for painters like Thomas Cole and landscape gardeners and authors like Andrew Jackson Downing to find an American audience for the ideas Birch and his immigrant contemporaries contributed to the rich ideological ferment of the new nation. These ideas would literally shape the American terrain, how it was viewed and used, and how it was represented on canvas and on the page.

Artistic Formation in Britain

The *Country Seats* was William Birch's third and final set of engraved views. His first and most popular view book, *Les Délices de la Grande Bretagne*, was completed at his house on Hampstead Heath outside London in 1791. The *Délices* was a gathering of British landscape images that reflected the taste for the picturesque that had become increasingly popular in Britain as the eighteenth century drew to a close. For the publication, Birch engraved paintings by artists as eminent as Sir Joshua Reynolds (1723–1792), the first president of the Royal Academy of the Arts (figure 1), and Benjamin West, Reynolds's successor in that position. Birch also reproduced the work of such important landscape specialists as Richard Wilson (1714–1782) as well as the work of amateurs and lesser-knowns. The *Délices* also marked the beginning of Birch's own career as a landscape artist—three of the images included were based on his own drawings (figures 2, 3, 4).

Birch's interest in landscape art—both graphic representation and work on the ground—arose in the vibrant artistic culture of London in the 1770s and 1780s. Birch had arrived in London in 1771 at the age of sixteen as an apprentice to goldsmith Thomas Jefferys.[6] He was a native of Warwick, the son of local physician Thomas Birch. He later attributed his initial interest in art to his father and older brother, and recalled his father as "fond of the arts" and as a patron of portraitist Thomas Worlidge (1700–1766).[7] Both Dr. Birch and his wife, Anne, née Russell, were natives of nearby Birmingham, famous for its role in the Industrial Revolution. Birmingham's industrial rise had many causes, among which may have been the high concentration of religious Dissenters in this unchartered town, and Birch's dissenter family members played a key role in his professional formation.[8]

Birch's father was a member of the Church of England and sat in (or at least rented) a prominent pew in St. Mary's Church in Warwick; his mother Anne was a Presbyterian who came from a family of Birmingham industrialists and merchants. Notable among Birch's maternal relations were Birch's uncle Thomas Russell (1696–1760), whose industrial activities reached the New World; he was among the founders of the first iron forge in the colony of Maryland, the Principio, located on a creek northeast of the mouth of the Susquehanna River. Russell's partners in the venture included Augustine and Lawrence Washington, George Washington's father and half-brother, respectively.[9] This familial connection with the colonies was furthered by the marriage of Birch's sister Ann (thirteen years his elder) to the Reverend Thomas Chase, a prominent Anglican clergyman in Annapolis

Figure 1. William Birch, after Sir Joshua Reynolds, *View from Richmond Hill*, engraving, 1788, published in Birch, *Délices de la Grande Bretagne*, 1791.

Figure 2. William Birch, *The Town and Castle of Warwick from Emscote*, engraving, 1789, published in Birch, *Délices de la Grande Bretagne*, 1791.

Figure 3. William Birch, *A Cave in the Chalk Cliffs at Margate*, engraving, 1790, published in Birch, *Délices de la Grande Bretagne*, 1791.

and Baltimore, whose son (by his first wife Matilda) was the revolutionary figure and U.S. Supreme Court Justice Samuel Chase (1741–1811). After his own emigration, Birch found these Maryland connections particularly important to his work as a landscape artist in the United States.

Another key family member in Birch's early life was Thomas Russell's son, Birmingham merchant and Unitarian reformer William Russell (1740–1818), whose markets for export goods, principally ironware, included North America. Russell was among the leaders of the Unitarian New Meeting in Birmingham and a supporter of minister and scientist Joseph Priestley (1733–1804). Along with Priestley, Russell and his brother were the principal targets of the 1791 mob violence generally known either as the Birmingham or Priestley riots, in which a dinner attended by the Russells, Priestley, and others commemorating the fall of the Bastille sparked an uprising in which the Russells' and Priestley's houses were destroyed.[10]

Many years before the riots, Russell intervened at crucial moments in Birch's early life as head of his mother's family, removing Birch as a young teenager from his home in Warwick to take him to Birmingham to attend to the young man's "education, which was scanty."[11] By the late 1760s when Birch came there, Russell had established an estate, Showell Green, southeast of the center of the city in an area where he owned agricultural lands. Showell Green was one of the first properties of the sort Birch would depict in his *Country Seats* with which he was intimately familiar (his parents lived in the center of Warwick). Birch recalled its state of development in the 1770s in detail in his autobiography:

[Russell's] elegant retreat [was] on Showell Green, three miles from Birmingham where I had formerly spent much of my time. He was a man of genuine taste. It was a handsome house upon an extensive flat of lawn; decorated with wide groups of shrubbery in the front, well-disposed. The kitchen garden [was] hid[den] from the eye in the general view within these groups of shrubbery. At the back of the house on the same extended lawn [there was] a large sheet of water embellished with gravel walks, lofty trees and shrubs, white seats, aviaries of American birds, &c. The whole [was] composed by himself in one general effect of harmony and beauty. On one side of the house, at a proper distance hid[den] with shrubs and trees, stood his well-stocked extended farm yard with a brick wall around it twelve feet high. His splendid farm [was] adjoining.[12]

Russell directed the beginning of Birch's professional life as well as his education. When Birch's mother arranged for the young man to be apprenticed to a Birmingham button maker, one of the many manufacturers of "toys" or small metal objects on which the city's economy depended, Russell chose alternatively to dispatch his young cousin to Thomas Jefferys in London in 1771, thus indirectly starting his artistic career.

Among the goods that Jefferys sold were small enameled objects, such as snuffboxes and watches, which Birch himself accurately described as "much in fashion" in the eighteenth century. The skills of fine metal-working and enameling that Birch learned during his apprenticeship became the foundation of the first phase of his professional career as an enamelist. By brokering an arrangement with miniaturist and enamel specialist Henry Spicer (1743?–1804), by which Birch would receive artistic instruction and Jefferys would give a share

Figure 4. William Birch, *The Garden Front of Kenwood, the Seat of the Earl of Mansfield*, engraving, 1789, published in Birch, *Délices de la Grande Bretagne*, 1791.

of the profits to the artist for goods sold by him, Birch began to shift his career away from trade toward the fine arts. Birch reports that he did "tolerably well" with Spicer and, by at least 1783, had established himself as an independent artist creating miniature enamel portraits, many of which were copies after works by Sir Joshua Reynolds.[13]

Enameling in Birch's era was not simply a matter of applying a brilliant translucent decoration to golden snuffboxes (figure 5). Enamel painting was recognized as an artistic medium and had been in regular use in Britain for small portraits since the seventeenth century. Birch took some pains in his own writing to detail the estimable artistic genealogy of the medium and its important practitioners in his era.[14] Domestic or "minor" arts and the fine arts came together in the creation of luxury metal containers and jewelry such as the pieces

Figure 5. Casket, painted enamel on copper, with baize lining and gilt metal mounts, English, ca. 1765–1775, Victoria and Albert Museum, London, from the collection of the late Charles Storr Kennedy, given by Myles B. Kennedy, C.424 to D-1914.

Thomas Jefferys purveyed in Covent Garden. Portraits and other figural representations were not, however, the only subject for enamelists like Birch.

He recorded the genesis of his *Délices de la Grande Bretagne* in the reproduction of a 1784 view by landscape painter Joseph Farington (1747–1821) of the high-arched bridge over the River Ouse in York (figure 6). Birch described this work, created for his patron Nathaniel Chauncey, as "a picture in the bold and correct style of Canaletto, clear and bright in effect. It was one of the most beautiful or perfect Enamels I ever painted." Birch went on to record that "the size of my plate was that which I engraved for my Delices De La Grande Bretagne, and which was the principal cause of my undertaking that work."[15] Although the shift in medium from enamel to engraving may seem illogical, it was conventional in the period to use a transfer print from an engraved plate as the basis for a figural enamel image, such as those used to decorate watches, small boxes, and similar objects sold by Jefferys and others. Thus, Birch moved only a short distance between media.

While the route from enamel painting to printed engravings that Birch followed was not the one taken by most landscape artists in the period, he was hardly alone in his interest in the representation of scenery or in the making of naturalistic gardens. In fact, as Birch's description of the genesis of his first set of views suggests, the taste for landscape went beyond paintings and engravings, and (as Birch's career also indicates) landscape art encompassed not only two-dimensional works, but also representations in the so-called minor arts, such as Birch's enamel and Wedgwood's pottery.[16]

Birch's interest in landscape art arose from the period of his career he spent in London in the 1770s and 1780s. His early career epitomized the British art world in the period in two respects—first, it had as one of its primary points of focus Sir Joshua Reynolds, and second, Birch was swept up in the contemporary British interest in landscape. Birch named Reynolds as his artistic "master" and reproduced his portraits in engravings and enamel (in jewelry settings) for wealthy and aristocratic patrons, many of whom were either the sitters or purchasers of the original paintings. As the president of the Royal Academy, Reynolds held a position at the apex of the social and professional hierarchy of British artists, having himself profoundly influenced the perception and place of artists in British society, shifting them away from craftsmen and toward professionals. Central to this move was Reynolds's notion (most publicly articulated in his lectures at the Academy) of the primacy of the intellectual basis of art. In other words, that technical and manual skill, while impor-

Figure 6. William Birch, after Joseph Farington, *Ouse Bridge at York*, engraving, 1788, published in Birch, *Délices de la Grande Bretagne*, 1791.

tant, did not lead to the creation of true art without "genius." Related to this was Reynolds's own social life, which served as an exemplar of appropriate behavior for young, aspiring artists like William Birch. Reynolds was "polished, wealthy, traveled, befriended by royalty and patronized by the great, sat at ease with London's wits and epitomized the glories which even an English painter could attain." Further, his "example made it difficult for contemporaries to place painters on a social level with carpenters and joiners, a common charge of the previous century."[17]

British artists, following Reynolds's example, may have been "befriended by royalty," but they depended on "the great" for their livelihood. In Birch's case, gentlemanly behavior and the patronage of gentry and aristocracy were crucial to the phase of his career in London. His work, both as an enamelist and landscape artist, depended on the direct support of either patron or subscriber. Birch later expected that the wealthy citizens of the new American republic would behave in a similar fashion, supporting his artistic work as a fulfillment of a public role accepted by social leaders. Unfortunately, this would be only intermittently realized, as is indicated by both the success of his first American view book, *The City of Philadelphia . . . in 1800*, and the failure to find a wide audience for the *Country Seats*.

In his autobiography, Birch's provides extensive detail of his social interactions with his wealthy patrons in London, establishing himself as an artist-gentleman and a man of taste in the Reynolds mold. Among Birch's most important patrons was William Murray (1705–1793), Lord Chief Justice and the first earl of Mansfield, who had retired to Kenwood, his estate north of London, at the time Birch knew him in the 1780s and early 1790s. In addition to buttressing his social and therefore professional identity, Birch's anecdotes relating to Lord Mansfield indicate his interest in landscape gardening before his departure for the United States, although there is no known executed work from this part of his career. At the time Birch knew Kenwood (he lived nearby on Hampstead Heath for eight years), the property included the mansion as remodeled by Robert and James Adam in 1764 to create the monumental south front Birch depicted in one of the three original views he included in the *Délices* (see figure 4). Humphry Repton's alterations to the grounds, however, were to take place after Mansfield's death and Birch's emigration to Philadelphia in 1794. Birch recounts that while on the earl's property, "I would often speak to his lordship of the improvements that might be made at Kenwood. He told me if he had been ten years younger he would submit to my taste in the entire new arrangement of his grounds."[18]

Les Délices de la Grande Bretagne

A KEY ASPECT OF Birch's early career indicates a point of divergence from Reynolds's artistic interests: landscape art.[19] Birch's *Délices de la Grande Bretagne* (1791) serves as an epitome of this interest in landscape as a fine arts subject and the connections between its practitioners and patrons in the British art world. In this first publication, in which he principally gathered views by other artists together with three original images of his own, Birch included the work of such important figures as Richard Wilson (1714–1782) and Thomas Gainsborough (1727–1788), who had done much to establish a popular interest in landscape as a subject for British painting. Although both were dead by the time of Birch's project, most of the artists whose work he compiled were his contemporaries and members of a generation of landscape specialists who practiced in the capital. Among these, Nicholas Pocock (1740–1821), known particularly for his images of marine scenery, exhibited more than one hundred views at the Royal Academy.[20] Joseph Farington, four of whose paintings Birch engraved (the largest number by a single artist), was also an elected member of the Academy, as were Philipp Jacob de Loutherbourg (1740–1812) and Philip Reinagle (1749–1833). Several of the paintings Birch reproduced were exhibited in the Academy between the late 1770s and 1790.[21] A number of the artists represented in the *Délices* were associated with other notable picturesque publication projects. Joseph Charles Barrow, whose 1790 view of Horace Walpole's famous country seat Strawberry Hill was included by Birch (figure 7), published a set of views of Twickenham in 1790, collaborating with George Isham Parkyns. In the United States, Parkyns's activities are an important parallel to Birch's own: as one of the few, if not the only, other immigrant professional landscape artist and designer active in the American early republican period, Parkyns would attempt (unsuccessfully) to publish a set of views of American scenery, and, as Birch documents, is responsible for the landscape garden for at least one country property on the Schuylkill River outside of Philadelphia. Parkyns was also involved with Birch in an abortive venture to establish an arts academy in Philadelphia in 1795.[22] Another artist on whom Birch drew for the *Délices*, Richard Courbauld, contributed to the *Picturesque Views of the Principal Seats of the Nobility and Gentry in England and Wales* (1786–1788).[23] Benjamin T. Pouncy (d. 1799) primarily worked as an engraver rather than a painter; his prints include the illustrations to Richard Payne Knight's famous *The Landscape: A Didactic Poem* (London, 1794), made from Thomas Hearne's drawings. More contributions to picturesque sets by artists whose work Birch chose to reproduce could easily be named.

Birch's first publication also indicates at least some of the engagements by amateurs with landscape art; such a group did not exist for all intents and purposes in the United States in the early republican period. Both of the amateurs whose work he reproduced were connected to him through patronage. Lord Duncannon, whose *View of Portsmouth and the Masts of the Royal George* was included, subscribed to the volume, purchased enamels from Birch, and appears in Birch's manuscript autobiography in the context of Birch's first introduction to the earl of Mansfield.[24] Duncannon's drawing of Blenheim was the source for an engraving (plate V) included in William Angus's 1787 *The Seats of the Nobility and Gentry in Great Britain and Wales*. The painting (*View in Wentworth Park, Yorkshire*) of the other amateur, "Mrs. M. Hartley," is noted in the description of the plate as "in possession of Lady Charlotte Wentworth," whom Birch also lists as the purchaser of several enamels after Reynolds.[25]

Birch's accounts of one patron, Nathaniel Chauncey

(1716/17–1790), a collector and antiquarian, amply demonstrate another kind of key engagement with the British landscape as well as the role this engagement played in Birch's formation. In this account of touring the countryside with Chauncey, Birch makes clear that his aesthetic education was both verbal and visual. Specifically, he learned to see and classify landscape types by their character-defining attributes, using an established vocabulary. He also acquired the picturesque habit of seeing the landscape as a "picture" or "scene":

> The greatest advantage I derived from [Chauncey's] friendship was in the summer season when he would wait my leisure to partake with him at his own expense the pleasure of a journey in his handsome vis a vis, which he had built for the purpose of travelling post. [There was] a seat for two in the back, and the whole front was one solid plate of polished glass, through which the enchanting scenery of Briton's Isle appeared as so many framed pictures. And knowing the country so well as he did, [he] took a pleasure in so directing the carriage as to surprise and astonish my delighted senses with everything new, beautiful, or picturesque, here and there driving up to the mansion or palace of some man of taste whose possessions were fraught with the finest specimens of the arts, in painting, sculpture and other objects of taste, [and] where I always found he was welcomed by a countenance of pleasure. It was thus travelling for a month, sometimes six weeks together, that stored my mind with a treasure well calculated for my profession.[26]

As this passage summarily demonstrates, the English eighteenth-century interest in and taste for landscape—perhaps best recognized under the familiar yet complex rubric of the picturesque—comprised, as much as any-

Figure 7. William Birch, after J. C. Barrow, *Strawberry Hill*, engraving, 1790, published in Birch, *Délices de la Grande Bretagne*, 1791.

thing, a way of understanding the native terrain: a way of both seeing and of articulating what is seen.

By the time of Birch's tours with Nathaniel Chauncey in the 1770s, British aesthetic theory and aesthetic landscape activities—which included such touring as well as garden-making—had developed several clear components and features.[27] The British effort in the period to classify landscapes and landscape aesthetics was strongly influenced by Thomas Whately's popular *Observations on Modern Gardening*, first published in London in 1770. For example, Whately classified different types found in the fundamental elements of a landscape, including rocks, wood, water, and ground. The enterprise of establishing an aesthetic typology relating to landscape had been ongoing in Britain throughout the eighteenth century. Among the widely read publications relating to this subject was Edmund Burke's 1757 *Philosophical Enquiry . . .* which redefined the sublime and the beautiful, representing essentially opposite aesthetic poles, including, for example, vast versus relatively small, and public versus private experience. By the latter part of the eighteenth century, the term "picturesque" had become inserted between the two poles of the sublime and the beautiful, sharing some attributes of both, and had acquired an association with that which is rough and rugged and what, "like a picture," was aesthetically pleasing. Among the artists whose work was seen as being "natural" in the sense of this sort of aesthetic was Salvator Rosa; while in London, Birch purchased a study by Rosa for his own landscape art collection.[28] The relationships between the perception of landscape in terms of the conventions of paintings by Rosa and others (most notably Claude Lorrain [1604–1682]), the making of "naturalistic" landscape gardens, and landscape painting are complex, but several useful observations can be made in relation to Birch's work and artistic formation in Britain.[29]

First, by the time Birch produced his *Délices de la Grande Bretagne*, the British market for landscape paintings and prints had broadened from the collecting of the work of sixteenth- and seventeenth-century Dutch, Italian, and French paintings and prints of landscape subjects (such as those Birch himself amassed) to a growing market in British landscape views in a variety of media.[30] Among the types of views for which there was an audience were those that featured country houses. Second, Britons increasingly traveled in their own country to experience it in aesthetic terms, as Birch and Chauncey did (this increasingly popular activity would be presented formulaically to a general readership by the Reverend William Gilpin in his *Three Essays: On Picturesque Beauty; on Picturesque Travel, and on Sketching Landscape* of 1792). Finally, if somewhat simplistically, a taste for the naturalistic, even the saliently wild in appearance, in both scenic touring and garden making, increased as the century wore on; Uvedale Price and Richard Payne Knight's polemic writings of the 1790s are typical culminations in this vein.

This was the landscape taste that Birch brought to the United States, and which informed his understanding of and appreciation for American nature, and the taste that is embodied in the *Country Seats*.

As has been suggested, Birch's *Délices* was one of many similar publications to appear in Britain in the second half of the eighteenth century; indeed, many of the artists whose work Birch reproduced were associated (as noted) with them. While many such volumes focused on particular categories of subjects—antiquities of a particular region, country houses, or the semi-wild scenery of a particular British area such as the Lake District—Birch's *Délices* brought together a variety of subjects, including townscapes, in addition to the categories already noted. In this, he assembled the variety of landscape "delights" of the British Isles, as his title and introduction adumbrated. Birch's gathering of landscapes also represents the range of aesthetic categories that came to be defined in Britain in the eighteenth century. His introduction announces the "grand characters of sublime" and the "lovely," or beautiful, and the "singular excellence of Britain for picture scenes," thus highlighting the triad of the sublime, the picturesque, and the beautiful. This theme is further developed by the assertion that "British landscape . . . comprehends whatever is beautiful in nature." To this essential superiority of the very fabric of the nation, further elaborated in his text (e.g., "perpetual verdure in our fields; the fine growth and vast variety of trees, with cheerful and various green in their foliage") is added the complementary achievements of humankind: "village and cottage scenes," "Roman, Gothic, and Druidal antiquities," "the ruins of our castles and abbeys," and "cultivation [that] ascends the tops of mountains." These assets unite to enable the climax of his general subject of the delights of Great Britain, at the end of his introduction, namely, "the palaces of nobility, from whose improvements the combination of art and nature can effect wonders." It is not surprising that Birch should claim that this wondrousness could be effected only by the forces of nature and culture exerted at the pinnacle of the British social hierarchy, but the specific examples of the "palaces of the nobility" and "elegant and costly structures" that Birch included in his publication bear closer examination relative to the subject of his final book, the *Country Seats*.

These buildings are never shown without something of their landscape garden setting, such as J. C. Barrow's view of *Strawberry Hill* (see figure 7), which features the rough-textured and tenebrous surroundings appropriate for Horace Walpole's "Gothick" mansion, or Richard Cooper's *Saltram, Devonshire*, shown in the context of its sunny lawns with clumped trees, evoking the character of Capability Brown's work there (figure 8).[31] In some cases, both the immediate surroundings of the country house and the "borrowed" area beyond are featured to the exclusion of the building, as in the first plate in the set of Reynolds's views from his upriver Thames villa at Richmond Hill (see figure 1). The plate and text that most clearly correspond to Birch's theme of the wondrous result of the artistic transformation of nature by the highest echelons of culture is his own *Garden Front of Kenwood*, showing the residence of his important patron and prominent jurist Lord Mansfield (see figure 4). In the image, the garden front created by Robert and James Adam dominates the allée of trees on the left portion of the plate, an echo of the stature of its owner that Birch evokes in his text. Despite the fact that "his Lordship's fine taste has ... embellished the whole with every thing of art that can adorn nature," Birch asserts that "the greatest ornament of the place is the noble possessor, to

Figure 8. William Birch, after Richard Cooper, *Saltram, Devonshire*, engraving, 1790, published in Birch, *Délices de la Grande Bretagne*, 1791.

whom Britain is so much indebted for the protection and improvement of its laws, as well as for his munificent patronage of the arts." Thus, Lord Mansfield's cultural contributions are ranked, with his more useful contribution to the law placed above the ornamental, however important the latter may be.

Like similar publications, Birch's first set of picturesque views found a relatively wide audience, garnering about 250 subscriptions for nearly 350 copies (booksellers and print dealers ordered up to a dozen). His subscribers ranged in social station from the king and queen to artisans and professionals, as well as a number of his fellow artists and members of the landed gentry. Birch would never again have such broad support for his printed work.

Despite the success of the *Délices*, several factors, including the death of Nathaniel Chauncey, Sir Joshua Reynolds, and Lord Mansfield in 1790, 1792, and 1793, respectively, caused Birch to decide to leave London in 1794. If he hoped for more opportunities to work as a landscape artist, both as image and garden-maker, the relatively rigid artistic hierarchy in London would have limited his opportunities to expand his practice.

The Philadelphia Scene and Early Success in America

Birch arrived in Philadelphia in 1794, part way through the ten-year residence there of the federal government established by the Compromise of 1790, before its departure for the new capital on the Potomac. Before, during, and for nearly a decade after the residency of the capital in Philadelphia, it was the former British colonies' largest and most prosperous city and most active maritime port, and in several respects the young nation's cultural capital. Within ten years after Birch's arrival there, however, Philadelphia's status relative to other cities of the young nation would have changed or be in the process of transformation. Some of these changes were dramatic and obvious, such as the departure of not only the federal, but also of the state government in 1800. By the close of the first decade of the nineteenth century, New York would surpass Philadelphia in population and the volume of its trade; Baltimore was similarly growing rapidly as a port city. Although these changes were yet to emerge in 1800, Birch nonetheless recognized the opportunity presented by the loss of both governments for the city to reshape its own image, and this determined the subject for his second set of views, the first to appear in the United States.

When Birch arrived in Philadelphia, he presented a letter of introduction from Benjamin West, the Pennsylvania-born painter who succeeded Sir Joshua Reynolds as president of the Royal Academy of Arts, to William Bingham (1752–1804), wealthy U.S. senator and merchant and center of the "Federalist court" in the city.[32] Birch would depict Bingham's city house on Third Street in his first American publication and his country house (Lansdowne) in the *Country Seats* (plate 5). Bingham hired Birch as a drawing master, and, using his income from this employment, Birch constructed a kiln and began to produce enamel portraits as he had done in London, the first of which were of Bingham and his wife, Anne. Birch also formed an alliance with Gilbert Stuart (1755–1828), who arrived in Philadelphia in the fall of 1794 shortly after Birch, and began reproducing Stuart's portraits of Washington, much as he had copied Reynolds's work in London, but with even more success. Birch found a ready market for enamels of Stuart's most famous portraits of George Washington produced in 1795–1796, including the full-length Lansdowne and the bust-length Athenaeum and Vaughan portraits, reporting that "I painted about 60 portraits" for which he could charge "from 30 to 100 D[ollars]" each. He also notes that most of the purchasers for these enamels were foreign visitors to the national capital.[33]

Most of these visitors (several subscribed to his *City of Philadelphia*) were diplomats who had come to Philadelphia as representatives of their governments. Among these was the Spanish envoy, Josef de Jáudenes y Nebot (1764–before 1819), with whom Birch shared the summer rental of a villa on the Schuylkill River; a view on this rented estate, Echo, would become the subject of one of the plates of the *Country Seats* (plate 6).

The Schuylkill River upstream from the settled parts of the city of Philadelphia would be the location of most of the properties and sites represented in Birch's *Country Seats*. At the time of his arrival in the United States, it was the most developed villa district in the young nation, perhaps rivaling only the Thames upriver of London for its concentration of suburban country houses. It was not unique, however, as the community of country seats on the upper east side of Manhattan (known as Hell Gate for its East River view) depicted in the *Country Seats* (plate 17) attests.

Thanks to John Lewis Guillemard (1764–1844), who arrived in Philadelphia as a British commissioner in 1797, Birch spent time at Solitude (plate 9), which Guillemard rented in the summer, and the two "visited about Schuylkill."[34] Birch describes several rural estates in his autobiography; some would be depicted in the *Country Seats*. Their stops included the property of Dr. William Smith (1727–1803), first provost of the University of Pennsylvania, near the falls of the Schuylkill River at the upstream end of the villa district in the period, and the nearby retreat of Judge Thomas Smith (1745–1809), a member of the Continental Congress and the half-brother of Provost Smith. Birch also spent time with Frederic Franck de la Roche, an aide to General Lafayette, at Fairy Hill, which would be depicted in Birch's view from Mendenhall's Prospect House (plate 18) along with the Laurels nearby. He describes the Woodlands (plate 14) as "first of note" among Schuylkill villas and noted that "it has a beautiful water scene towards the Delaware" and that the "ground is spacious and elegant." The property of Lansdowne (plate 5) is characterized as "a fine spot," with "a good house upon it," but Birch disapproved of the specific location of the dwelling, asserting that it "was placed too far back from the water."[35]

Birch also noted Eaglesfield, a 1799 estate, which, while not depicted in the *Country Seats*, was painted by Birch's son Thomas in 1808. He records that it was "a very engaging spot of much beauty laid out by Mr. Parkyns near Solitude."[36] Parkyns, already mentioned as J. C. Barrow's collaborator on a 1790 set of views of Twickenham, was one of a group of professional landscape specialists and designers who, like Birch, emigrated to the young nation's capital in the 1790s in pursuit of opportunities they anticipated in America. None met with unmitigated success, not even the best known of this cohort, Benjamin Henry Latrobe (1764–1820), whose designs for the Center Square Water Works and Bank of Pennsylvania are represented in the *City of Philadelphia* and whose Sedgeley for merchant William Cramond was included in the *Country Seats* (plate 15).

Parkyns's American work and associations are instructive in this respect. Like Birch, Parkyns had engraved picturesque views before his emigration, had also published designs for landscape gardens, and was the probable architect for the villa at Eaglesfield as well as the landscape gardener for the property.[37] Parkyns was the only other artist whose American work was included in Birch's didactic art collection at Springland, his own property on the Delaware, in addition to Birch's own "Landscape, the effect of Sun upon the Dew," which would become the basis of his print for Echo (plate 6) in the *Country Seats*.[38] Birch also records that Parkyns made a "sett of drawings" for a publication on country estates "which he called the Tour of Schuylkill."[39] This project, which never appeared, could have been a factor in Birch's decision to issue the *Country Seats*.

In addition to the "Tour of Schuylkill" Parkyns may have been contemplating, he attempted to publish another set of views, the plan for which he had formulated by the time of his arrival in Philadelphia in 1794 or very shortly thereafter.[40] Only four of these were issued; two showed Washington, D.C., one Annapolis, Maryland, and one Mount Vernon.[41] The project attracted too few subscriptions, and Parkyns returned to Britain in 1801. Like Parkyns, immigrants William Groombridge (1748–1811) and John James Barralet (ca. 1747–1815), whose landscape subjects included oils of views on the Schuylkill, in the area around Washington, and in New York, struggled to find an American market for their work. Although they remained in the United States, both died in the early years of the nineteenth century without achieving the success they had emigrated to obtain.[42]

Despite Parkyns's and others' difficulties in finding support for American views, Birch seized the moment of change in Philadelphia in 1800 to publish *The City of Philadelphia in the State of Pennsylvania*. He recorded the mercantilist promotional nature of the volume in his autobiography, accurately asserting that "No other work of the kind had ever been published by which an idea of the early improvements of the country could be conveyed to Europe, to promote and encourage settlers to the establishment of trade and commerce."[43] The tone of cheerful nationalist hyperbole that Birch used in the *Délices* in regard to the natural advantages of Britain for "picture scenes" was transformed from word to image in Birch's second set of engravings, which presents its subject as a modern, civilized, commercial and residential city. Birch successfully garnered subscriptions from the city's merchants, bankers, and politicians, as well as those outside the city who wished to demonstrate the advancement of American culture more generally. Thomas Jefferson was among these, and Birch attests that during the president's administration, the publication "lay on the sofia [*sic*] in his visiting room at Washington until it became ragged and dirty, but was not suffered to be taken away."[44]

Landscape Designs and Picturesque Tours

BIRCH'S SUCCESS AS A landscape artist after his emigration was not limited to the publication of *The City of Philadelphia*. In his American career, he was able to expand his professional practice to landscape design, and the *Country Seats* presents some of this work, among other subjects. In his autobiography, Birch records that the profits earned from sales of *The City of Philadelphia* at the turn of the nineteenth century allowed him to proceed with construction of his own country property, Springland, located on the Delaware River, and to tour his adopted country.[45] Birch wrote extensively, if somewhat indirectly, about the character of his improvements at Springland, which he first purchased in 1798, and created a number of images in connection with his designs there, two of which were incorporated in the *Country Seats* (figures 9, 10, 11; frontispiece [plate 2] and plate 20).[46] Most of his discussion of Springland comes in the form of a poem in two sections and is the clearest account of his landscape design approach. The format and tone of the poem recall such works as Richard Payne Knight's *Landscape, A Didactic Poem*. The first section of the poem describes two visits to the property before he made any changes there; the second, like Knight's, is intended to educate the reader and was entitled "Springland Improved as a Lesson in Landscape Gardening." In the first section, an account of two visits he calls "the Discovery of Springland," he rapturously catalogues the flora, fauna, and physiographic features of the site in an iteration of American wonders. For example, he notes the "gilt-eyed frog," the "massy ches[t]nut" and "rare botanic plants." On his second visit he is caught in a thunderstorm that brings down a massive tree, evoking both the sublimity of American nature and its physical dangers.

The final didactic section uses the assets described on his first visit and moderates the more dangerous natural aspects of the site suggested in the account of his second visit. He begins by evoking both the talent of the landscape gardener and the *genius loci* to neutralize natural American dangers ("Now genus let your wand be rais'd; / Expell the Vipers, with there nestling brude, / The poison Vine, that throws its deadly grasp, / Around the Verdent Oke; the deadly shoemac, / From disperseing its poisonous influance in the Aire") and goes on to direct the reader to "let Nature be your god; she has charms with all her / Fa[u]lts that Art can never give." As stated, this was not a new idea and did not necessarily invoke an aesthetic of what in the introduction to the *Country Seats* Birch calls "wild unregulated nature." The lines that follow, however, articulate a light-handed approach: "Trim not your bows away with wanton hand, / Let cautious taste reserve them for effect; / Spoil not your broken ground with too hasty levelling." He goes on to exhort his gardening reader to "advantage take from the roughest / Rudeness chance has given, so let the refinement / Of your taste work its way,"

Figure 9. William Birch, *The View from Springland Cot*, watercolor on paper, ca. 1798–1805, Collection the Library Company of Philadelphia.

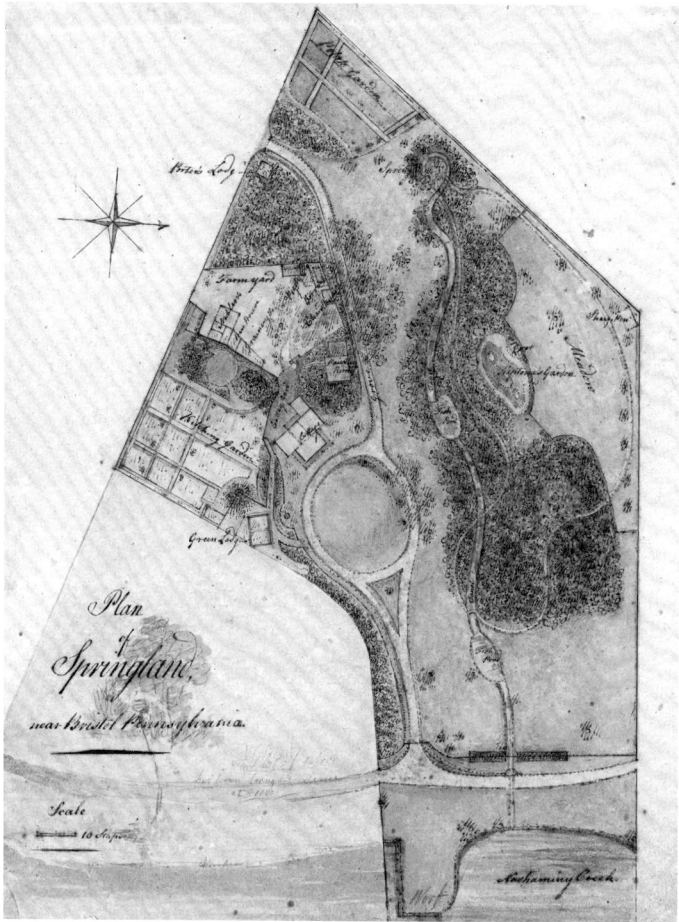

Figure 10. William Birch, *Plan of Springland*, watercolor on paper, ca. 1798–1805, private collection.

and concludes that "Thus with wholsom caution" was Springland "Improved."⁴⁷

In addition to enabling his "improvements" at Springland, the profits from the sale of the first edition of the *City of Philadelphia* allowed Birch to indulge himself in some picturesque touring of his adopted country in the first decade of the nineteenth century. He journeyed north to New York City and its vicinity, noting that he received there "friendly reception and politeness" and that he visited Gouverneur Morris (1752–1816) at his family's estate Morrisiana, which occupied a large portion of what is now the Bronx and Westchester County, New York. He also "paid a visit at the seat of Mr. A[rchibald] Gracie, and viewed several elegant retreats on the North [i.e. Hudson] River"; the merchant Gracie's property (now known as Gracie Mansion) and those adjacent to his on the East River on the upper east side of Manhattan are represented in the *Country Seats* as "York Island" (plate 17).⁴⁸

More important for understanding Birch's career as a landscape designer, however, were his journeys south into Delaware, Maryland, and northern Virginia, "calling on my route upon those characters most distinguished in my former connection [and] with those I wished to improve my knowledge of." Chief among the former was Birch's relative by marriage Samuel Chase, who opened a number of doors for him in Maryland. There, the traveling artist was received warmly by politicians such as former Maryland governor John Mercer, by wealthy landowners, including Charles Carroll of Carrollton, and, not surprisingly, by Chase and Birch relatives, including Birch's own nieces, who lived in Annapolis and whom he had never met, as well as the widow of his cousin Thomas Russell.⁴⁹

Birch included several descriptions of the Maryland and Virginia countryside in the accounts of his travels—as in his descriptions of his encounters with the property he would develop as Springland, these are revealing accounts of the application of the aesthetic principles he had acquired in England. Most of these accounts relate directly to the situation of country houses, either finished or in construction at the time of his travels between 1800 and 1810. In Annapolis, Birch was asked by Judge Jeremiah T. Chase (Samuel's cousin, 1748–1828) to accompany him on a ride to his country house outside the city to discuss possible improvements to it.

Arriving at the property, Birch remarks with approval upon its situation on an "elevated flat of beautiful retirement enriched by a water scene below." In what seems an offhand remark, he adds that his vantage point improves the "elephant appearance" of the State House dome, causing it to "effect more of the Roman structure [St. Peter's]."[50] This seemingly simple comparison reflects the way that he learned to see what was around him, based in part on the formal conventions of Claude's paintings. Birch brought his mental Claude glass across the Atlantic and used it to understand the New World landscape.[51] Unlike his predecessors, and, more significantly, unlike most of his American contemporaries, he represented what he saw using both words and images, and he did so to a degree that was largely unrivaled at the time.

Broadly speaking, Birch's perception of the American landscape was "picturesque" in the sense that he was in the habit of defining what he saw using the Claudean formulas he had learned in London. He was not alone among the citizens of the young nation in this ability; many educated Americans were familiar with these formulas. Others were not, however, as adept as Birch in applying them, and, more important, were not much in the habit of using them to understand the American landscape. Nor were many of them accustomed to classifying it using aesthetic terms with much facility.[52]

In contrast, Birch had acquired a very specific aesthetic vocabulary in Britain that he could use to categorize what he encountered on his travels. For example, he opens his description of the Annapolis view by qualifying it as a "wild and picturesque scene." Like his comparison of the Maryland State House and St. Peter's in Rome, this apparently straightforward assertion has several implications. By using "wild" and

Figure 11. William Birch, *Springland: The Artist's Residence*, enamel on copper, after 1798, Courtesy of the Pennsylvania Academy of the Fine Arts, Philadelphia. Bequest of Constance A. Jones.

"picturesque" together, he reveals not just his familiarity with the British aesthetic theories of the last decades of the eighteenth century, but his positive interest in this untamed aesthetic. In a similar vein, Birch dubs the countryside near Green Hill, the property of his cousin's widow, Ann Russell, as "wild beautiful."

Green Hill was located northeast of the mouth of the Susquehanna River in Cecil County, Maryland; the picturesque surroundings of a nearby property on the southwest side of the river, outside the town of Havre de Grace, receive particular attention in Birch's manuscript. Birch's visit to Mount Pleasant, the estate of ironmaster Samuel Hughes, provides the subject for his most detailed landscape description. Here he again avows an appreciation for the undeveloped, both in juxtaposition to and as a lesson for the garden. Birch relies on the Burkean sublime, as Jefferson and many before him had, to characterize the scale of his American surroundings. And, while his account is more detailed than many contemporary examples, he reaches a point where, as with his contemporaries, his descriptive abilities fail him and he merely alludes to the larger view:[53]

> After mounting a hill of winding turns through rugged rock and overhanging shades of darksome gloom, rising by degrees to upland heights, to a level with the Gods; [one was] launched at once upon an extended flat of verdant green, enriched with cooling fountains and murmuring cataracts from neighboring heights [which were] screened from the sight by woody foliage of the scene; wile from the uplifted dwelling on the lawn, [one] look[ed] down upon a soft picture blended in air, over tops of forest trees on the descending hill, a wide extended view of the Chesapeake Bay in its richest form, and most splendid effect.[54]

He concludes by noting the relationship between garden art and what he sees around him. His final allusion in this passage notes the desirability of the contrast between the more "natural" aesthetic he sees in abundance around him and the more refined (or "beautiful," in Burke's sense) areas of the garden: "[This view] completed at once the feeling of a student in the arts for the admiration of nature . . . [and] the beauties of the surrounding scenes . . . afforded me the finest lessons for landscape gardening, seeing the wilds of nature so richly offering to the leading hand of Art, those beauties which in Europe form the enchantment of every polished ground."[55]

In the course of his tours, Birch traveled through northern Virginia, in part to visit his daughter Albina, who married Alexandria merchant Guy Atkinson in 1803.[56] Birch probably made the drawing that would become the basis for his view of Mount Vernon (plate 7) about this time. While in the area, he visited and commented in his autobiography on Arlington and Woodlawn, which were in the process of being built by Washington relatives and in-laws: Martha Washington's grandson George Washington Parke Custis (1781–1857), and Lawrence Lewis (1767–1839, George Washington's nephew who married Eleanor Parke Custis, George Custis's older sister.[57]

Birch writes that he had tried to dissuade G. W. P. Custis from building on the intended location on the property (now Arlington National Cemetery) because of the "difficulty of attaining comforts upon the site." Birch goes on, however, to describe the view from it and the specific location of the house and its aesthetic relationship to its surroundings approvingly, noting that

> the scene around it was splendid and elegant . . . [and] took in a complete view of the city of Washington with the arm of the Potomac, the surrounding hills of Georgetown, the rich decoration of Mason's Island with a full birdseye view of his own farm at the foot of Arlington. [Custis] had built the two wings of his house, which, with the hill they stood upon, were an ornament to every elegant situation within the city limits of Washington. If anybody's taste and perseverance can surmount the difficulties of rendering its spot comfortable, it must be his own.[58]

Birch's account of Woodlawn is less laudatory. While he acknowledges both "the more beautiful situation than that of [Mount Vernon]" and the house's design—"he had built two wings, which were handsome elevations"—he relates that Lewis "was at a stand whether to go on with the mansion or not, [due to] a defect in the plan." Birch saw the garden as an important intermediary between the house and its undeveloped surroundings: a middle term, like the picturesque, that shares certain qualities with those on either side. In typically cryptic fashion, he expresses this by identifying the "defect" as the placement of the house "too much upon the precipice of the Bank" of the Potomac, which he decries as "an error often committed in this country." Birch defines this common American mistake: "The builder in his choice for a spot to build on places himself upon the point most beautiful for the scene, saying there shall be the seat or the door of the house forgetting the advantage of lawn, or that too much familiarity with beauty wears to indifference, whereas as more domestic adoption of [natural] beauty by art [seen] from the house would reserve the principal beauty of the situation and the advantage to be taken in the descent before it."[59]

Birch himself had several opportunities to avoid this error and to ameliorate the surroundings of houses already built through landscape design commissions that came to him through his travels in the south. In contrast, he is not known to have received any design commissions in Philadelphia. Birch provided architectural and landscape designs for patrons in Delaware and Maryland, but none of his design work is known to survive. Similarly, and in contrast to his plan and views for Springland, neither do any drawings associated with his built designs, with one exception. Montebello, located in Baltimore, was one of the properties Birch included in the *Country Seats* (plate 13). Birch's responsibility for the project is documented in his letterpress description ("the house was built by Gen S. Smith, from a plan and elevation by Mr. W. Birch, the proprietor of this work"), and by a surviving plan and an accompanying watercolor that became the basis of the plate (figures 12 and 13).

Birch records two commissions in Delaware, in country houses near Wilmington. In contrast to his

Figure 12. William Birch, *Montebello*, watercolor and ink over graphite on paper, The Baltimore Museum of Art: Presented in Honor of Calman J. Zamoiski, Jr., President of the Board of Trustees (1977–1981), by his fellow trustees BMA 1980.165.2.

dismissive remarks on the location of Woodlawn, he praises the hilltop site of the house of James Tilton (1745–1822), a medical doctor and former member of the Continental Congress, as a "fine situation." Birch stayed with Tilton "some days" and furnished a plan for the grounds, reporting that "I made him a drawing, by his desire, for which he rewarded me handsomely, and [he] was well pleased with it." Tilton made an introduction to Delaware Congressman Caesar Rodney (1772–1824), "who had a lot next to [Tilton's] more favourable for improvement." Birch supplied a design for the grounds "which he approved, but I believe was not adopted."[60]

Birch's best-documented commission came through Henri-Joseph Stier (1743–1821), a refugee from Belgium who after spending time in Philadelphia and Annapolis, brought his family in 1801 to a property in Bladensburg, Maryland, approximately two and a half miles northeast of the District of Columbia line. Birch's garden design for Riversdale, the name of the property, was commissioned in 1803, shortly

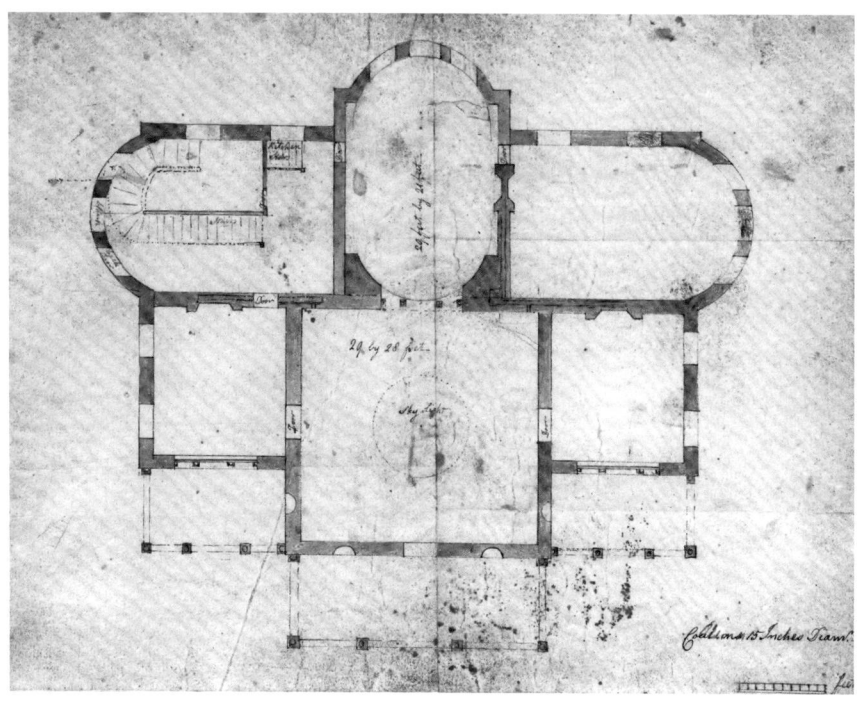

Figure 13. William Birch, *Plan of Montebello*, pen and ink, and brush and wash on paper, ca. 1798–1799, The Baltimore Museum of Art: Presented in Honor of Calman J. Zamoiski, Jr., President of the Board of Trustees (1977–1981), by his fellow trustees BMA 1980.165.1.

before Stier and his son returned to Belgium. Having hired Benjamin Henry Latrobe as the architect for the house, Stier left the property with his daughter Rosalie, who had married a member of the Calvert family, the former lords Baltimore and prominent Maryland landowners.[61] Stier's correspondence with his daughter indicates his ideas for the property and landscape gardening; most important for understanding Birch's career, Stier articulates the fundamental relationship between landscape representation and design: "I believe it is absolutely necessary to have an architect who is also a painter to design the landscape plan, and I believe Mr. Birth [sic] is the best one for the job. The grounds have great potential for a beautiful landscape."[62] Rosalie and George Calvert officially engaged Birch to create designs in the fall of 1805, and a year later he completed plans that included an artificial lake on the south side of the house.[63] Birch neither supervised work on the property nor in fact ever saw it after he completed his plan (which is not known to survive). He reports that he thought "very little was done" according to his design, but details of the garden in Rosalie Stier Calvert's correspondence suggest that at least the water feature to the south was completed; further, it is possible that a system of paths with Brownian "clumps" of trees and shrubbery on the north side of the house were Birch's design.[64]

Birch credits an introduction by Samuel Chase for a commission at Hampton, the vast estate in Towson, Maryland, owned by Charles Carnan Ridgley (1760–1829). There, Birch designed a portion of the landscape garden, although again no plan survives. Hampton later became the subject of another plate in the *Country Seats* (plate 4), and the engraving could easily represent either some portion of his design or relate to it. In a brief reference to the project, Birch alludes to the relationship between landscape painting and landscape gardening: "Hampton is beautiful and richly deserved the adoption of Art in its improvement, I made several designs for that purpose which were approved."[65]

Country Seats

Birch's only mention of the publication of his third and final book-length work appears in his autobiography in connection with his visits to country houses on the Schuylkill River in the vicinity of Philadelphia. He notes disparagingly that "I have published a set of *Country Seats*, the principal plates of which, so far as it continued, were the seats on the Schuylkill River. The work extended to twenty plates, the only work of the kind yet published, but want of encouragement stopped its progress."[66] This "want" was so dire that Birch included no subscription list for the *Country Seats* in his autobiographical writings. Thus, in contrast to his other publications, we have no clear indication of the number of copies he sold.[67]

Birch was not alone in the "want of encouragement" of his book of views of American scenery; in fact, the outright failure to find support sufficient to sustain a professional career or the evident struggle to do so marked virtually all similar contemporary efforts, including landscape paintings that depicted American scenery and other attempted sets of views aimed at the domestic market. Between the Treaty of Paris and the War of 1812, the stories of such ventures (and the careers of landscape artists generally) can be called tales of woe rather than songs of victory, even though this period saw the production of landscape views for a domestic American audience in greater numbers than ever before. Among the more successful artists (by comparison with those who failed utterly) was the already noted George Isham Parkyns, who did sell some landscape paintings, and received, like Birch, at least one landscape gardening commission.

Prints of American scenery had been produced before Birch issued either *The City of Philadelphia* or the *Country Seats*, including most notably, *Scenographia Americana* (London, 1768), whose twenty-eight folio prints were the most ambitious such publication, not least in the size of its engravings. It was, however, intended largely for a British "home" audience rather than for colonial purchasers.[68] Leaving aside the work of specialists such as Birch and Parkyns, landscape images produced for American audiences either before the Revolution or in the early national period were almost never produced or viewed in isolation. Instead, they most often appeared in one of two contexts. Before the rebellion, they conventionally were produced as portrait backgrounds or occasionally as promotional images or map marginalia; after, they were published in the context of early national magazines, where they accompanied or were accompanied by (often lengthy) print articles or descriptions. Thus, landscape images were primarily illustrations, and therefore secondary, to the text context in which they appeared, just as the earlier American landscape images were subordinate to the main pictorial subject of the portrait sitter.

The work of Charles Willson Peale is instructive in regard to both portrait backgrounds and views published in early national magazines. In two representative examples, views of the Schuylkill River near Philadelphia are associated with meanings that went beyond what was visible in the image itself. In the case of Peale's *John Dickinson* of 1770 (figure 14), the falls of the river upstream of Philadelphia (the practical limit of the villa district on the Schuylkill) are shown in the background of the portrait of this important figure in the resistance to the Stamp Act.[69] The image of the falls is not, however, merely ornamental. Instead, it is emblematic of an important moment in the public embrace of colonial protest, since the Fort St. David's fishing company, near the site of the falls, served as the location where Dickinson was first revealed as the anonymous author of the *Letters from a Farmer in Pennsylvania*, an important document in the protest against the Townshend Duties, and would have specifically reminded contemporary viewers of this.[70]

One of the most important outlets for American landscape views after the Revolution was the early national illustrated periodicals published in the late eighteenth and early nineteenth centuries, beginning with the *Columbian Magazine*, which originated in Philadelphia in 1786. Peale's August 1787 *Columbian Magazine* view of the Gray's Ferry floating bridge (figure 15) is deceptively simple in comparison to the anonymous poem "Verses Upon Grey's Ferry" that accompanied it. The contrast between the relatively crude style of the image and the complexity of the associations packed in the poem is typical of the relationship between landscape view and text in these periodicals, and underlines the difference between Birch's work and those of his American predecessors.

The anonymous poem quite dramatically demonstrates the chasm between the complex literary notions invested in American place and the crude visual representations that accompanied them. The poem also gives an indication of the complexity of the ideas associated with the Schuylkill River, the primary locus of the sites Birch chose to depict in the *Country Seats*. The poem addresses the arts, country life, and the river—all themes he would take up—and, while it focuses on the Schuylkill, the ideas expressed in it were applicable to all of the suburban territory that he represented in the *Country Seats*.[71] The verses begin with a complaint by the muses to Apollo ("bright god of day") of their neglect by a "race unpolish'd." They plead for a "soft retreat, [and] some airy mansion chuse, / and there from rage protect the injur'd muse." The god responds by creating, "on his western way," "A winding vale . . . secure from summer's heat, and winter's storms; / The rocks and woods adorn its bending sides, / And Schuylkill here in gentle murmur glides." The poet addresses Gray's Inn and the rocks around it, from which a view to the south was available:[72]

Figure 14. Charles Willson Peale, *John Dickinson*, oil on canvas, 1770, Courtesy of Historical Society of Pennsylvania Collection, the Atwater Kent Museum of Philadelphia.

> Above the reft two rocks of equal size,
> With their aspiring fronts assail the skies;
> The one ascended, yields the glorious sight,
> Where the Delaware and Schuylkill's streams unite;
> The other by the hand of art array'd,
> Affords a mansion's shelter and a forest's shade.

Figure 15. Charles Willson Peale, *Grey's Ferry Bridge*, published in the *Columbian Magazine*, 1787, Courtesy the Library Company of Philadelphia.

The author then turns to both the qualities of the river upstream and its inspirational properties for American poets (but not, it should be noted, for American painters):

Beyond these rocks, the vale obliquely bends
To where the woodland's airy mount ascends,
There down the steep a fountain gently glides,
Or, swell'd with rain, rolls on its foamy tides,
Then through the vale in wild meanders flows,
Now hides its limped head, now kindly shows.
Oft have Diana and her virgin train,
Tir'd with the pleasures of the open plain,
In this recess their weary limbs repos'd,
And to soft winds their softer parts expos'd;
Here oft her train have round their goddess stood,
While naked she enjoy'd the silver flood;
The Paphian Queen, and all her winged loves,
For this have left their high Indian groves,
Here, with the muses passed their flowing hours
Near the cool stream or in the shady bow'rs;
While the Sweet nine their golden harps have strung
And Waller's verse on Sacharissa sung.
Thus did Apollo for his choir prepare
A seat removed from public strife and care,
For which the muse in gratitude has brought
To the Schuylkill's bank the Greek and Roman thought.
There, to her Barlow, gave the sounding string,
And first taught Smith, and Humphries how to sing.

Several themes central to the *Country Seats* are embodied in this poem. Notable among these is the country retreat, the "seat removed from public strife and care" as a locus of the arts (here presented as poetry rather than painting). Also crucial is the continuity of American civilization with ancient culture: the alighting of "Greek and Roman thought" on "Schuylkill's bank." Here the ancient Roman notion of *otium* and its association with rural retirement is invoked: Horace, Virgil, Pliny the Younger, Columella, and other ancient authors may seem immeasurably remote chronologically from the villas Birch depicted, but they were neither intellectually nor culturally distant from the eighteenth- and early nineteenth-century owners of those properties. *Otium*, a difficult term to translate directly into modern American English, connotes the peace and quiet, the rest, the positive "nothing"-ness of country life. Most of plates of the *Country Seats* reflect this idea—there is little human activity or even presence in most of them. Both the letterpress description and the engraving of the Solitude (plate 9) embody this sense directly: "Here a pleasing solitude at once speaks the propriety of its title. Upon further research the solitary rocks, and the waters of the Schuylkill add sublimity to quietness."

The notion of *otium* is featured in Birch's introduction to the *Country Seats*, which, like the opening text to the *Délices de la Grande Bretagne*, presents the main themes of Birch's publication. In contrast to his first publication, the application of "art" to "nature" is now his principal consideration rather than a secondary theme; it is presented in ways that are reminiscent of, but significantly different from the formulation in the *Délices*, particularly in respect to the terms Birch uses to discuss those who carry out this application. The association of country life and the arts in the anonymous author's 1787 poem are echoed here, beginning, in his somewhat jumbled first sentence, by linking the developing state of the professional practice of the arts in the young country ("the fine arts are, as to the American Nation at large, in their infancy") with rural residence. More important for his own professional interests, he asserts that the application of art to nature in the specific locus of the country seat "supported by the growing wealth of the nation" (that is, applied by those with sufficient funds) will be conducive to "form[ing] the National character favourable to the civilization of this young country, and establish that respectability which will add to its strength." Here, "wonders" will not be wrought by nobility in palaces in the countryside as in Britain; instead, wealthy citizens will set an example that will aid in the advancement of the establishment of the young nation's culture and status among other countries. The artistic sophistication of the owners or builders of the properties included in the volume is noted in the letterpress at several points: for example, the "legitimacy of the General's taste" is an important point of the description accompanying the image of Mount Vernon (plate 7). Equally, the grounds of the Woodlands (plate 14) are "laid out in good taste" and "paintings & c. of the first masters embellish the interior of the house, and do credit to [owner] Mr. Wm. Hamilton, as a man of refined taste."

Birch's notion of the "fine arts" and his declaration that they will aid in the formation of the new culture are typical of the public rhetoric in the period, which was often preoccupied with the self-conscious effort of nation-building. Birch's writing differs in one crucial point from this public rhetoric and indicates a likely cause for the lack of contemporary support for the *Country Seats*. Stated somewhat simplistically, art, as opposed to craft, was often viewed as outside this enterprise of cultural construction, if not antithetic to it. The "fine arts" were indeed often viewed with suspicion generally in the early national period due to their association with the dissipated luxuries and corruptions of older, European countries.[73] An elite individual artist's (interior) "genius" was frequently deemed less significant than an artisan's contribution to the collective task, if it was not downright suspect.[74] In his autobiography, Birch bemoaned the lack of support for the "fine arts" in the United States in the early republican period. He noted that the "country is new and flourishing. The mechanical arts are at their highest pitch, but the fine arts are of another complexion," and that "the distinction between the arts and the fine arts is not generally understood." He placed the "basis of the fine arts [as the] superiority of ideas expressed from the superior senses of the mind," and also denigrated "unmeaning amateurs" as incapable of producing "fine arts."[75]

The ambiguities and hesitations that bedeviled many American artists in the early nineteenth century are expressed in many period documents. In an example close to Birch in Philadelphia, the remarks of George Clymer, first president of the Pennsylvania Academy of the Fine Arts, at the 1807 opening of the institution include a number of contemporary attitudes. He begins by asserting the presence of artistic "genius" in the United States and presents the Academy as an example of the advancement of American civilization. He dwells extensively, however, on the need for discipline in the arts in an argument against the excesses manifest by corrupt European nations (that is, the Italian baroque and the rococo). His discussion indicates some of the pejorative associations with the arts in the period:

> Between simplicity and refinement, or, if you will, luxury, the question has been frequent and undecided; but if luxury be a consequential evil of the progress of our country, a better question perhaps it would be, How is it to be withstood? Where an unrestricted and unoppressed industry gains more than simplicity requires, the excess, as it cannot be pent up, will be employed upon gratifications beyond it—how retain the cause and repress the effect? Philosophy and the laws would here teach in vain! Where a constantly rising flood cannot be banked out, the waters should be directed into channels the least hurtful—so ought the exuberant riches, which would incline towards voluptuousness, to be led off to objects more innoxious—even to those of greater purity and innocence; those that will not pamper the senses, but rather amuse, if not instruct the understanding; and it may, with some truth be observed, that those who carry the whole fruit of an assiduous and successful toil to the common hoard of national wealth, undiminished by any waste of it, but on the few wants of simplicity, contribute with most effect to the refinements or luxuries, to which in their practice they seemed most averse.
>
> Such being the consequence of a growing opulence, the alternative would be, not as between simplicity and luxury, but between the grosser and more refined species of the latter. Where is the room then for hesitation in the choice?[76]

Shortly after this lukewarm endorsement, Clymer links the artisanal image of the artist both with Reynolds's concept of genius and with collective, nationalist effort: "the mechanick arts, we mean those of the more ingenious and elegant kinds, not failing of the inspiration, the workman in them is converted into an artist, and partake of the common benefit."

Although many artists struggled in the early national period, including most of Birch's fellow British immigrants, he was among the few effectively to incorporate a sense of communal purpose—"common benefit"—in his *City of Philadelphia*.[77] Therefore, it is hardly surprising that he presented his subject in the *Country Seats* as serving this same cultural project.

Birch's introduction to the *Country Seats* proclaims the literally natural superiority of the nation that is its subject in a manner similar to the opening of the *Délices de la Grande Bretagne*. Echoing his first publication, he also provides a kind of catalogue of features that make up this superiority, declaring that "the face of nature is so variegated" and "sportive" (that is, varied and various, using "sportive" in its sense of the spontaneous appearance of a new form in a plant), and noting the "broken Precipices

Figure 16. Cornelius Tiebout, *The Seat of Henry Livingston, Esq. at Poughkeepsie*, from the *New York Magazine, or Literary Repository*, 1791, Courtesy the Library Company of Philadelphia.

and Crags," "the curious and sublime of the Forest Trees," the "Cataracts and Rivers," "the blue Capt Mountains," and "the deep, retired, and darksome Vallies."

In contrast to the *Délices*, however, this catalogue of the elements of "wild unregulated" (American) nature is not presented merely as the subject for "picture scenes." As the plates and their accompanying descriptions demonstrate, this is an important aspect of their purpose here. However, Birch states that "it would be impossible to do justice in a work, *such as this is intended to be*" (emphasis added)—that is, a work on American country residences—without presenting "some plates" of American nature and "some scenes which decorate the ground *and form the choicest Pictures of themselves . . .* [to] be given separately, as highly necessary to form a *full and correct idea of the American Country Residence*" (emphasis added).

Two crucial points are implicit in Birch's discussion of the setting of rural estates. The first is that the American country seat is carved out of the wild. This was hardly a new concept, but Birch made a subtle yet crucial shift from American precedents on the subject. A representative earlier example can be found in the view and accompanying description of the *Seat of Henry Livingston, Esq. at Poughkeepsie* on the Hudson River that appeared in May 1791 in the *New York Magazine, or Literary Repository* (figure 16). The description presents a rare appreciation in the period for the undeveloped nature that Birch would celebrate nearly twenty years later: "Although the mansion is far from magnificent—although no artificial fountains sprinkle the parterres, or statues of pagodas are seen from the gardens, nor any extraordinary effort of expence exhibited; yet nature, in her kindliest mood, has undulated the hills around, smoothed the terrene where the buildings are erected, laved the shores with the majestic Hudson, and made the whole delightful."[78]

The key difference between the point of view embodied here and Birch's is that the surroundings are represented as, in essence, already improved for the use of the owner. This is very clear in the view itself, in which the hallmarks of the domestication of the Hudson River landscape are featured: cleared, fenced land, neat buildings, and regularly spaced trees of orderly settlement take literal center stage and smooth surfaces predominate. In contrast, Birch presents the rural property as the means of contextualizing undomesticated American nature and therefore rendering it understandable (and expunged of dangers, according to his Springland poem). As his earlier passage and his descriptions of visits to estates in Maryland and Virginia suggest, he saw the proper place of the garden as both a reflection of undeveloped land and an intermediary between wilderness and settlement.

Equally significant for the *Country Seats* is the role of the picturesque understanding of landscape as represented both graphically and verbally in the formation of "a full and correct idea of the American Country Residence." The subject of the susceptibility of American nature to "picture scenes"—which had been the principal preoccupation of the *Délices* in regard to Britain—is definitely in evidence in the *Country Seats*, but put to the purpose of Birch's main subject. The centrality of landscape art, and its role in forming a country property according to the principles of landscape painting and in seeing it and its surroundings in those terms, is never stated directly in the *Country Seats*. The primacy of the aesthetics of the setting relative to the design of the dwelling is, however, clearly stated in the second paragraph of the introduction, in which he asserts that the "advantages of a Country Residence ... consist more in the beauty of the situation, than in the massy magnitude of the edifice."

The aesthetic qualities of the sites and the relationship of the property to landscape views are also recurring topics in the letterpress descriptions of the plates in the *Country Seats*. For example, Lansdowne (plate 5), outside of Philadelphia, is found on the "bank of the Pastoral Schuylkill, a stream of peculiar beauty." Equally, the Woodlands (plate 14) "is charmingly situated on the winding Schuylkill" and "commands one of the most superb water scenes to be imagined." Sedgeley (plate 15) is found "amidst romantic woods" as would be appropriate for a Gothic-style residence—the picturesque is featured here in its association with roughness and irregularity in both house and setting. The most effusive text again focuses on the Schuylkill and accompanies the engraving of Belmont (plate 16), which depicts the view from the property toward the east. Birch states that "it is impossible for the artist, who has fixed his attention upon the various beauties of the Schuylkill, to leave the study of its charms. Here you pass from the wild romantic scene; the rugged stone with wood and water bound to expand the sight from this high lifted lawn, to view in open space the world below ... and the verdant banks of the fluid mirror that reflects the sky."

Most of the views of the properties themselves are organized according to the pictorial conventions Birch learned in Britain in the latter eighteenth century.[79] One plate that diverges from these conventions, however, does suggest Birch's effort to create a new, American work and fulfills his promise to depict "scenes which decorate the ground." More than any other image in the *Country Seats*, *Echo* (plate 6) embodies the effort to depict the raw, "wild unregulated" American nature of the volume's introduction in a way that was new and different from the conventions Birch learned in Britain. As a whole, the visual scene has a mysterious quality, in part because the light is mostly screened from the viewer. Further, the lack of human figures removes a sense of scale. The plate is simultaneously awkward and remarkably original.

The accompanying description explains his depiction of a small portion of the grounds at the expense of the house (which is "of no note") and the river view by recalling the site as a revolutionary encampment of Washington and his troops. He thus associates national history with his image of undeveloped American countryside. By this association, Birch establishes one of the fundamental points of the *Country Seats*: an equation of the significance of American nature with that of national heroes. Again, this was not an entirely new idea; rather, it was a substantial development of the "interchangeability of the face of American nature with the faces of exemplary Americans" exemplified, for example, in a 1791 call in the *Massachusetts Magazine* for "likenesses of celebrated Americans; or views of publick buildings, bridges, or remarkable natural curiosities."[80] Birch's reference to the presence of Washington's troops in the landscape is the sort of emblematic maneuver that Peale was conducting in his *John Dickinson*, in which a nationalistic narrative or value was being deliberately associated with an image of American landscape. Here, however, there is a subtle yet monumental shift: the association of a heroic event is made without resort to the visual representation of any human presence whatsoever. Thus the landscape, if not American nature itself, is made nearly as epic as the human actor.[81]

The text for *Echo* also elaborates a theme first suggested in the text accompanying the view of Hoboken (plate 3), namely, its "command" of the "extensive view." This military metaphor for intervention would have been a familiar reference to the act of settlement for his American audience. The crucial discrepancy between his approach—an interest in the undeveloped landscape—and that of his contemporaries, is clear in the accompanying plate. The character of Birch's "improvement" is further clarified in the text accompanying the view of Echo which vaunts the site as "rich in every wild luxury which nature can afford to the plastic hand of art." This wild scene represents the raw materials out of which a landscape garden could be fashioned.

The contrast between this plate and the previous print, showing Lansdowne, also on the west bank of the Schuylkill, is remarkable in its demonstration of the distance Birch had traveled from his work in England. In its composition and the representation of the house, the Lansdowne image closely resembles the depictions of country houses in the British sets of views with which Birch was familiar, such as the view of Saltram (see figure 8) he included in the *Délices*. It relies on an established tradition, but the plate representing Echo, the "Sun reflecting on Dew," is very much an experiment in depicting raw American nature itself.

In the same vein, the final engraving in the volume, the second view of Springland (plate 20), reflects the sense of the adaptation of this raw American nature as a landscape garden. Birch entitles the engraving the "view from the Elysian Bower," thus, boosterishly signaling the paradisial nature of the site. In contrast to the completely enclosed sense of the view on the property at Echo, an opening to the setting is clearly visible in the form of a small sailboat in Neshaminy Creek in the background.

It should be noted, finally, that Birch's work also encompassed a complementary approach to the landscape typical of the period, much in the vein of Hoboken's "command" of its Hudson River vista. Today, this approach seems antithetical to his celebration of undeveloped American wildness embodied in the view of Echo and its incorporation in the landscape garden embodied in the last plate of *Country Seats*. In his image and account of Fountain Green (plate 8), also on the Schuylkill, the building of the new canal figures prominently. While such a quasi-industrial development might seem to run counter to Birch's aesthetic, his letterpress predicts that the canal, "if ever finished, will be a great ornament to the place." The print furthers connects the house and the canal: the composition is neatly divided in two by a prominent tree, but a small, arched bridge leads over the canal to the towpath at the right. Beyond this is the river itself, and the wooded rises on its far shore are shown in an undeveloped state. The canal is both part of the garden (as the text suggests) and a crucial intermediary between settlement and the larger landscape. The attitude expressed here may seem to contradict the appreciation of the undeveloped evinced throughout the *Country Seats*, but it reflects a contemporary understanding of "internal improvements" (public works such as roads, canals, lighthouses, water systems, turnpikes, and other activities like the large-scale surveying of western land), including projects Birch knew personally like Philadelphia's Center Square Waterworks, shown in the *City of Philadelphia*. These Jeffersonian-era projects were literally the stuff of nation-building, and were perceived as the means of creating a new country that would rival more established (European) civilizations. The *Country Seats* captures a contemporary understanding of these "improvements," when they were viewed as neither ugly nor physically damaging to the environment, in contrast to modern attitudes. Birch's text and engraving show, instead, his contemporaries' positive outlook on these undertakings.[82]

Suburban Villas

The nationalistic tenor of the publication (which starts with its title and title page) is reflected in Birch's selection of properties and the ways in which he represents them both verbally and visually in the *Country Seats*. The vast majority of houses shown were built or substantially remodeled after the Revolution. Mount Vernon is an exception but was clearly included for its association with Washington, just as the Delord-Sarpy mansion (plate 12) was included to stand for the Louisiana Purchase of 1803. Lansdowne, completed about 1773, was likely included for its "handsome and correct plan." The motive for the view of the Echo estate has already been explored. Birch's view of the U.S. Capitol under construction on his title page was clearly intended to serve his nationalistic theme. The two wings of the building are shown before the completion of the central dome. The sawyer in the midst of crates of construction materials in front of the incomplete portion of the building emphasizes the act of construction of a seat of national government. Birch shows none of the physical surroundings of the building beyond a simple earth platform, but contemporary viewers would have been familiar with the undeveloped (country) condition of Washington in the period, which was more extensively documented in a drawing by Birch from the period (figure 17). The plate is dominated by an eagle and flag, and the typography of the title emphasizes the "United States." This page proclaims a significant role for Birch's subject in nation building.

In the engraving representing Belmont (plate 16), the mid-eighteenth-century house is excluded, presumably because, unlike Mount Vernon, it would not have appropriately represented the taste Birch saw as exemplary for the new nation. Instead, the view is taken from the vicinity of the house, as is made clear by the bollards visible in the foreground. What one sees instead of the house, as Birch's letterpress states, is the view of the city, itself located in a wild context ("the big metropolis in the woods"), taken from its suburbs, the locus of "the chequered country with her merchants' seats." This view and its description indicate a key aspect of this epitome of Birch's subject. He did not attempt to represent the entire "expanded republic" geographically in the *Country Seats*, in contrast to the relatively comprehensive approach he had brought to both the *Délices*, which included views of sites from the Dover coast up to Scotland, and that in the *City of Philadelphia*, whose views systematically covered the settled areas of the city from its southern and northern boundaries on the Delaware River west to Center Square. Instead, he focused on the area of the highest concentration of urban development and political power of the new nation: the area from New York City to Washington, D.C. (the area corresponding roughly to

Figure 17. William Birch, *View of the Capitol, Washington, D.C.*, watercolor on paper, ca. 1805, Library of Congress.

the range of his travels in the early nineteenth century). A source contemporary with the *Country Seats* described much of this area vividly as the zone of a "pendulum of national activity, which must long vibrate (perhaps for ever) between Baltimore, Philadelphia, and New-York; a chain of commercial cities, unparalleled in history, whose vigorous impulse is already accelerated by the bold ramification of turnpikes and canals."[83]

Further, and just as important, Birch's nationalistic selection clearly excluded remote rural properties or any outside the urban range he chose. Yet, the descriptions in his autobiography of the surroundings and situation of country properties he visited in Maryland and Delaware demonstrate that he certainly had other options. Despite his admiring descriptions of Thomas Jefferson and visits with him at the White House, Birch rejects any image of the country life of the yeoman farmer or the frontier settler; instead, he chose to represent in his selections the locus of *otium* as the obverse but inseparable partner of *negotium*, or business.[84] The ideal of country life as it was understood by ancient Roman authors and by Anglo-Americans (both colonials and citizens of the young republic) was one that was directly related to city life: in other words, this ideal was found in the suburbs.[85]

Birch emphasizes the communal quality of the American suburban landscape in several views in the *Country Seats*: *York Island* (plate 17) depicts this most completely in showing the East River villas within their landscape setting (an "extended country" in which the "innumerable seats" shine "like so many stars in the firmament"). An area in the northern section of the Schuylkill district is seen in *Mendenhall Ferry* (plate 18), and picturesque touring of the vicinity is suggested by the emphasis in the view and the letterpress on Mendenhall's Prospect Lodge, a "house of public entertainment" in the left foreground. By placing the tavern in shadow and literally marginalizing it, he emphasizes the view of the opposite shore, where Fairy Hill and the Laurels sit like jewels in their natural(istic) Schuylkill landscape.

Similarly, in the view of Sedgeley (plate 15), the house dominates the foreground, but this dwelling is complemented by another in the distance. The viewer's eye is directed to this second building by a line of light in the left foreground, and by the roof lines of Sedgeley itself. Birch identifies this tiny structure on the opposite bank of the Schuylkill as Lansdowne, and he describes Sedgeley as being in its "neighbourhood." This is something of a distortion, since the latter stood much closer to Mount Sidney (plate 11); this proximity is invoked in the letterpress that notes Mount Sidney's "sylvan scene" as mingling "with the romantic wilds of Sedgely." In fact, the Solitude (plate 9) was much closer to the latter on the opposite shore. Both the plate and the description, however, give the impression of the Schuylkill and its country estates as a single extended landscape garden in which one property served as an aesthetic asset to another. Birch's account of Sedgeley presents the river itself—not seen in the plate—as a docile connecting thread, and a natural ornament: "[Lansdowne] is seen in the distance on the opposite side of the river, whose gentle stream courses lowly and humble, amidst romantic woods, gently descending lawns and caverned rocks." The larger landscape (and the view) is thus made up here by a succession of suburban estates.

Virtually all of the properties Birch depicted or described as part of these shared suburban landscapes can be characterized as the "merchant seats" noted in the Belmont view description. These were not, however, the only kind of property that Birch included in the *Country Seats*. Although all of the properties represented were suburban in the sense of their physical proximity to an American city, they can be divided roughly into two categories based on the relationship of the properties to the income of their owners. The first type comes closest to the sort represented by Saltram in that they constituted very large land holdings that provided the primary source of income for their owners, largely through agriculture. The second are more properly called villas—relatively small rural holdings that do not represent the principal livelihood for the owner or owners.[86]

Hampton (plate 3), located north of Baltimore in Maryland and the property of the Ridgely family, perhaps best epitomizes the first category, although Mount Vernon also properly falls under this rubric. At the time of Birch's publication, Hampton included not only extensive agricultural lands but also a productive iron forge in its 25,000 acres. This sort of property was the closest to the "palaces of the nobility" which Birch had included in the *Délices*, and in fact, as Birch's *Country Seats* plate clearly indicates, the design of the building is deliberately palatial, recalling the large, central cupola of Castle Howard to invoke a family tie claimed by Hampton's builder on his mother's side. The land holdings of the Stevens family in northern New Jersey, shown in the image of Hoboken (plate 4), were also prodigious.

The vast majority of the properties that Birch depicted, however, fall into the second, "villa" category, even those such as the contiguous Schuylkill estates of Lansdowne (plate 5) and Belmont (plate 16), which, at the turn of the nineteenth century, each included nearly 300 acres. While these provided some agricultural income, their owners did not depend on them as their main source of support. Springland itself did not provide an income for Birch, although he hoped that his garden there would bring him design commissions. It is the relative number of these suburban villas represented in *Country Seats* that most significantly differentiated the publication from precedent British examples. True, like the "palaces of the nobility" (as well as grand estates such as Stourhead developed by wealthy nonaristocratic members of the upper classes), both suburban villas and suburban villa districts in America had British parallels and antecedents. Reynolds's view from his upriver Thames villa included in the *Délices* (see figure 1) represents one such property, and, arguably, the Thames afforded the most significant precedent for the suburban villa districts developed along the rivers of Philadelphia, New York, and other American cities.

While these connections can easily be traced, the subtle differences between the roles that large country seats and suburban villas played in British culture and those that they represented in the nascent American culture are nonetheless crucial, and Birch's *Country Seats* is significant for emphasizing the villas. One of the most salient of these differences is the discrepancy between the political roles played by large American and British country estates. For example, while the owner of Hampton at the time of the publication of the *Country Seats*, Charles Carnan Ridgely (1760–1829), held several important political positions, including that of governor of the state of Maryland (1815–1817), Hampton was never the political power base that a large estate in Britain was for its owner. Similarly, with the abolition of primogeniture in the United States, the conveyance of country estates intact from one generation to the next was not a given as it was in Britain.

Further, and perhaps more important, the vicissitudes of the mercantile basis of the American urban economy in the early republican period are neatly encapsulated by the history of the development of the riverside villa districts (particularly along the Schuylkill) and the transfer of individual properties within these districts. Of all the properties depicted in the *Country Seats*, only Hampton remained relatively intact as an estate into the twentieth century in the hands of a single family.[87] The fate of most of the rest of the rural residences shown by Birch charts the risks and rapid changes of fortune inherent in mercantile activities (and in American commercial society) in the early republic.

Like many of the men whose houses appear in Birch's second set of American engravings, the seemingly simple phrase "in trade" and the contemporary occupational description "merchant" mask a complex and risky world of finance and commercial speculation that made and broke (and sometimes remade) many American fortunes in this period and represented an important facet of the new American economy and culture. Samuel Smith (1752–1839), whose Baltimore house Montebello (plate 13) Birch both designed and depicted, depended on privateering for a sizable portion of his fortune, as did William Bingham (named as the owner of Lansdowne and whose townhouse Birch depicted in the *City of Philadelphia*).[88] Both these men went on to become prominent citizens of the new republic: Smith was a U.S. Representative during Birch's first years in Philadelphia, and later became a U.S. Senator during Thomas Jefferson's administration. Bingham was a founder of the Bank of North America, a member of the Continental Congress and the Pennsylvania Assembly, and also a U.S. Senator. Americans like Bingham and Smith could begin their careers as merchants and style themselves as gentlemen after they had accumulated enough money, escaping the stigma—common in Britain—that was attached to someone who had once been "in trade."

Not all early national merchants held onto their fortunes. Like most of his cohort, Bingham also invested heavily in land speculation: he owned two million acres in New England, much of which is now in the state of Maine. Other land speculators in the period fell victim to the risks inherent in the venture; the most famous financial failure of the early republic was Robert Morris (1734–1806), whose grand, unfinished mansion Birch represented in the *City of Philadelphia*, and whose Schuylkill estate, the Hills, was sold at auction in the effort to satisfy his debts. Morris, a U.S. Senator and the great financial backer of the Revolution, was broken by a term in debtor's prison after being brought down by land speculation. Morris's failure threatened the stability of at least one of the owners of the properties Birch depicted: William Cramond, who hired Benjamin Henry Latrobe in 1799 to design his Schuylkill River house Sedgeley (plate 15).[89] Within a decade, Cramond lost the property to satisfy debts for an investment gone sour after his business partnership had gone into bankruptcy.[90] New York merchant Archibald Gracie, whose property is featured in plate 17, similarly lost his country residence (in 1823).[91]

The impermanence of American mercantile fortunes was one cause of the difference between patronage for the arts in Old World and the New, and in part it explains Birch's frustrations in finding the support he wished for the *Country Seats*. In the context of such impermanence, art and architectural and landscape designs were not commissioned as enhancements to an estate passed on undivided to succeeding generations. Instead, they expressed the achievements and interests of individuals, if not their identity or claim to it. This was a key difference between the British precedents that Birch knew and the properties that he showed in the *Country Seats*: the degree to which they were centered on the individual owner. For example, Birch's patron,

Figure 18. William Birch, *View of China Retreat*, watercolor on paper, ca. 1798, Library Company of Philadelphia.

diplomat and China merchant Andreas Everardus van Braam Houckgeest (1739–1801), built a country house on the Delaware in the 1790s which he named "China Retreat" and crowned by a cupola in the form of a miniature pagoda (plate 19; figure 18).[92]

Birch himself emphasizes the important role of mercantile capital in one of the longer letterpress descriptions in his publication—he narrates the view from Belmont as a sort of progress, beginning from the "wild romantic scene" of "rugged stone with wood and water" and moving to the "world below." In this is found the "big metropolis in the woods," and, in counterpart to this, the "chequered country with her [the city's] merchants' seats" as well as the "bustle of agriculture" (representing the economic role of country life). The suburban districts Birch depicted along the Schuylkill and Delaware rivers outside of Philadelphia, as well as those along the East and Hudson rivers outside of New York, were dominated by villas enabled by new, mercantile money.

Birch's *Country Seats*, for all of its immediate failure to find as many subscribers as had his earlier sets of views, provides us today with a remarkably evocative commentary on his chosen subject. The cultural vision that he suggests throughout his letterpress and in the careful structuring of his graphic images reveals a new and essentially American understanding of landscape taste. The villa districts shown in his engravings have parallels, as he knew, in the Old World (especially in his own London), but Birch understood, and more important, clearly represented, the cultural significance of the American mercantile conjunction of *otium* and *negotium* and how this was already shaping the American landscape. His insights into how these villas and their landscapes presented the material, cultural accomplishments, not just of their owners, but also of a young nation, continue to resonate even today.

Notes

1. A. J. Downing, *The Architecture of Country Houses* (New York: D. Appleton, 1850; reprint, New York: Dover, 1969), xix.
2. For example, in his 1822 *Address Delivered before the Philadelphia Society for Promoting Agriculture* (Philadelphia: Printed by order of the Society), banker Nicholas Biddle wrote disparagingly of the deplorable lack of agricultural development lands in Pennsylvania, describing as a "calamity" the failure to subject "unbroken wilderness, the habitual hunting ground of savages" (p. 18) to the plow. On the rhetorical experience of American landscape, see Gregory Clark, *Rhetorical Landscape in America* (Columbia: University of South Carolina Press, 2004).
3. On the *City of Philadelphia*, see Emily T. Cooperman, "William Russell Birch (1755–1834) and the Beginnings of the American Picturesque" (Ph.D. diss., University of Pennsylvania, 1999), chapter 5.
4. Hampton was listed on the National Register of Historic Places in 1966 and is open to the public as a National Historic Site. George Washington's Mount Vernon remains one of the nation's most visited historic sites. The Solitude survives on the

grounds of the Philadelphia Zoo. Belmont is open to the public as one of the historic houses in Philadelphia's Fairmount Park. The Woodlands, on the grounds of a rural cemetery since the 1840s, is listed as a National Historic Landmark. Gracie Mansion, which has served as the residence of the Mayor of New York City, is also open to the public as a historic site and is listed on the National Register of Historic Places.

5. On contemporary landscape painters and landscape imagery, see Cooperman, "William Russell Birch," chapter 6.

6. On Jefferys, see Arthur G. Grimwade, *London Goldsmiths, 1697–1837: Their Marks and Lives*, 2nd ed. (New York: Faber and Faber, 1982), 560–561.

7. An edited and annotated version of Birch's manuscript, which survives in two known versions and which he entitled "The Life and Anecdotes of William Russell Birch, Enamel Painter . . ." will be part of a forthcoming monograph publication sponsored by the Athenaeum of Philadelphia, edited by Lea Carson Sherk and annotated by Cooperman. The manuscript also exists in typescript in several public institutions: in Philadelphia at the Historical Society of Pennsylvania (HSP) and the Free Library of Philadelphia, and in the New-York Historical Society in New York City. Hereafter the manuscript will be cited as Birch's "Life," with page references to the Free Library copy, which, although in a single volume, is paginated to reflect the two volumes of the original from which it was drawn. Citations will therefore refer to volume. Spelling and other corrections reflect the edited version as it will appear in the forthcoming publication. Birch, "Life," 2: 8–9.

8. For a concise account of the multitude of factors in Birmingham's economic growth in the eighteenth century, see Eric Hopkins, *The Rise of the Manufacturing Town: Birmingham and the Industrial Revolution* (Gloucestershire: Sutton Publishing, 1998), 4–5.

9. On the Principio Forge, see Michael Warren Robbins, "The Principio Company: Iron-Making in Colonial Maryland, 1720–1781," Ph.D. diss., George Washington University, 1972, and Henry and William G. Whitely, "The Principio Company," *Pennsylvania Magazine of History and Biography* 11 (1887): 63–68, 190–198, 288–295.

10. See R. B. Rose, "The Priestley Riots of 1791," *Past and Present* 18 (Nov. 1960): 68–88.

11. Birch, "Life," 2: 5.

12. Birch, "Life," 2: 6–7.

13. Birch, "Life," 1: 36.

14. Birch, "Life," 1: 1–4.

15. Birch, "Life," 1: 9; Birch probably referred here to the size of the engraved view rather than the full copper plate, which is larger (approximately 6 in. high and 6 5/8 in. wide). The dimensions of the image are roughly 3 by 4 in.

16. Wedgwood's Frog Service, made for Catherine the Great of Russia, is the best-known example of such decoration. See Hilary Young, ed., *The Genius of Wedgwood* (London: Victoria and Albert Museum, 1995), 134–148.

17. Neil Harris, *The Artist in American Society: The Formative Years, 1790–1860*, 2nd ed. (Chicago: University of Chicago Press, 1982), 11.

18. Birch, "Life," 1: 20. Repton's work at Kenwood, in 1793, was for the second earl of Mansfield, William Murray's nephew. See John Summerson, *The Iveagh Bequest: Kenwood, A Short Account of its History and Architecture* (London: Greater London Council, 1974), and George Carter, Patrick Goode, and Kedrun Laurie, *Humphry Repton, Landscape Gardener, 1752–1818* (London: Victoria and Albert Museum, 1982).

19. Reynolds disdained naturalistic landscape gardening as an art in his thirteenth Discourse, which addresses the arts in their imitative relationship to nature. He states that "Gardening, as far as Gardening is an Art, or entitled to that appellation, is a deviation from nature; for if the true taste consists, as many hold, in banishing every appearance of Art, or any traces of the footsteps of man, it would then be no longer a Garden." Joshua Reynolds, *The Works of Sir Joshua Reynolds, Knt. . . .*, 2 vols. (London, 1797), vol. 1, p. 284.

20. David Cordingly, "Pocock, Nicholas (1740–1821)," *Oxford Dictionary of National Biography*, Oxford University Press, September 2004; online edition, May 2007, http://www.oxforddnb.com/view/article/22425, accessed September 8, 2007.

21. Algernon Graves, *The Royal Academy of Arts: A Complete Dictionary of Contributors and Their Work from Its Foundation in 1769 to 1904* (London, 1905–6; reprint, Bath: Kingsmead Reprints, 1970), 1: 166, 301; 2: 87.

22. The organization, dubbed the Columbianum, is principally documented in the scholarship of the American artist Charles Willson Peale, who was among the most prominent participants. See, *inter alia*, Lillian B. Miller, ed., *The Selected Papers of Charles Willson Peale and His Family* 2 (New Haven: Published for the National Portrait Gallery, Smithsonian Institution, by Yale University Press, 1983), part 1, 102. Documents and commentary on the Columbianum appear on 102–113. See also *The*

Constitution of the Columbianum, or American Academy of the Fine Arts ... (Philadelphia: Printed by Francis and Robert Bailey, 1795).

23. *Picturesque Views of the Principal Seats of the Nobility and Gentry in England and Wales* (London: Harrison and Company, 1786–1788).

24. Frederic Ponsonby (1758–1844), Viscount Duncannon, later third Earl of Bessborough, was also a patron of Reynolds. See Birch, "Life," 1: 21–22.

25. Mary Hartley (dates unknown) is listed as an amateur landscape painter in standard biographical sources. Quote from the *Délices* appears in the description for plate 5. One enamel was of the Earl of Mansfield, and two were of her brother, the Marquis of Rockingham. Birch, "Life," 1: 6, 7.

26. Birch, "Life," 1: 17–18.

27. The date when Birch's friendship with Chauncey began is unknown, but if his claim is true that he introduced Reynolds and Chauncey (Birch, "Life," 1: 17), then he knew the latter by the mid-1770s, the date of Reynolds's portrait of him. See David Mannings, *Sir Joshua Reynolds: A Complete Catalogue of His Paintings* (New Haven: Published for the Paul Mellon Centre for Studies in British Art by Yale University Press, 2000), 130.

28. Cooperman, "William Russell Birch," appendix C.

29. On the relationship between Claude's paintings and picturesque formulas, see Malcolm Andrews, *The Search for the Picturesque: Landscape Aesthetics and Tourism in Britain, 1760–1800* (Aldershot: Scolar Press, 1989), 24–38.

30. Birch's own collection included landscapes by late sixteenth- and seventeenth-century Dutch, Flemish, Italian, and French painters. Among the better known artists represented were Jacob van Ruisdael (1628/29–1682) and Jan van Goyen (1596–1656), as well as Guido Reni (1575–1642). See Cooperman, "William Russell Birch," appendix C.

31. For a thorough documentation of the subject, see Sarah R. Katz, "Horace Walpole's Landscape at Strawberry Hill," *Studies in the History of Gardens and Other Designed Landscapes*, 28, no. 1 (2008), 9 ff.

32. On Bingham and his town house, see Richard G. Miller, "The Federal City 1783–1800," in Russell F. Weigley, ed., *Philadelphia: A 300-Year History* (New York: W. W. Norton, 1982), 177, and Margaret L. Brown, "Mr. and Mrs. William Bingham of Philadelphia," *Pennsylvania Magazine of History and Biography* 61 (July 1937): 286–324.

33. Birch, "Life," 1: 40. Surviving enamels of Washington by Birch can be found in several American public collections, including the Walters Art Gallery and the Maryland Historical Society, both in Baltimore, the Cleveland Museum of Art, Middleton Place in Charleston, South Carolina, and the R. W. Norton Gallery in Shreveport, Louisiana. On the Washington portraits, see Carrie Rebora Barratt and Ellen G. Miles, *Gilbert Stuart* (New York: Metropolitan Museum of Art, 2004), 129–183.

34. Birch, "Life," 1: 46. See H. G. Lyons, "John Lewis Guillemard (1764–1844)," *Notes and Records of the Royal Society of London* 3 (April 1940–September 1941): 95–96. Guillemard also subscribed to Birch's *City of Philadelphia*.

35. Birch, "Life," 1: 46–47.

36. Parkyns's designs were for merchant James Egglesfield Griffith. See Kathleen A. Foster, *Captain Watson's Travels in America, the Sketchbook Diary of Joshua Rowley Watson, 1771–1818* (Philadelphia: University of Pennsylvania Press, 1997), 41–46. The house stood on the west side of the Schuylkill River north of Solitude.

37. Foster, *Captain Watson's Travels in America*. On Parkyns, see Judith Ann Hughes, "George Isham Parkyns," in Edward Nygren, ed., *Views and Visions* (Washington, D.C.: The Corcoran, 1986), 276–277. In addition to engravings, Parkyns had published in London in 1793 his original "Six Designs for Improving and Embellishing Grounds," which appeared as an appendix to Soane's *Sketches in Architecture*. See Eleanor M. McPeck, "George Isham Parkyns: Artist and Landscape Architect, 1749–1820," *Quarterly Journal of the Library of Congress* 3 (July 1973): 171–182; and A. A. Tait, "The American Garden in Milburn Tower," in Robert P. McCubbin and Peter Martin, eds., *British and American Gardens in the Eighteenth Century* (Williamsburg, Va.: Colonial Williamsburg Foundation, 1984), 84–91.

38. See Cooperman, "William Russell Birch," appendix C. A watercolor of the same subject by Birch survives in the collection of the Corcoran. Birch described Parkyns's view as a "scene sublime and finely painted." See Cooperman, chapter 4 and appendix C, and "Belfield, Springland and Early American Picturesque: The Artist's Garden in the American Early Republic," *Studies in the History of Gardens & Designed Landscapes* 26, no. 2 (2006): 126.

39. Birch, "Life," 1: 47.

40. E. McSherry Fowble, in *Two Centuries of Prints in America, 1680–1880: A Selective Catalogue of the Winterthur Museum Collection* (Charlottesville: Published for the Henry Francis du Pont Winterthur Museum by the University Press of Virginia,

1987), 88, describes his intent as an "updated series of views as an alternative to the now all-too-familiar sets from *Scenographia Americana.*"

41. Several of these views were republished in London in 1804 by Richard Phillips. See Fowble, *Two Centuries of Prints in America*, 88, 89.

42. On Groombridge, Barralet, and their contemporaries, see J. Hall Pleasants, "Four Late Eighteenth Century Anglo-American Landscape Painters," *Proceedings of the American Antiquarian Society* 52 (1942): 187–324, and Cooperman, "William Russell Birch," chapter 6.

43. Birch, "Life," 1: 48.

44. Birch, "Life," 1: 49.

45. Birch, "Life," 2: 11.

46. See Cooperman, "William Russell Birch," chapter 4, and "Belfield, Springland, and Early American Picturesque," 123–126.

47. The portion of Birch's "Life" that includes the poem is included only in the transcriptions in the collection of the Historical Society of Pennsylvania. For the full text of the poem, see that volume.

48. Birch, "Life," 2: 23.

49. Birch, "Life," 2: 12, 15, 18–20.

50. Birch, "Life," 2: 19.

51. On Claude glasses and mirrors, "optical devices which took various forms" in order that the viewer see the landscape in the visual terms of a Claude painting, as well as similar "knick-knacks," see Andrews, *Search for the Picturesque*, 67–73.

52. Author Charles Brockden Brown might be noted as an exception to this. On Brown's writings on the picturesque and related aesthetics, see Beth L. Lueck, *American Writers and the Picturesque Tour: The Search for National Identity, 1790–1860* (New York: Garland, 1997), chapter 2; and Robert Lawson-Peebles, *Landscape and Written Expression in Revolutionary America* (New York: Cambridge University Press, 1988), chapter 7.

53. On the limits of contemporary landscape description see Robert Clark, "The Absent Landscape of America's Eighteenth Century," in Mark Gidley and Robert Lawson-Peebles, eds., *Views of American Landscapes* (Cambridge: Cambridge University Press, 1989), 81–99.

54. Birch "Life," 2: 13–14. Samuel Hughes was one of the most important producers of cannon and other ordinance for the colonists during the Revolution. In 1802, Hughes purchased Mount Pleasant, a property of more than 800 acres (grown to nearly twice that by Hughes within a decade) to the southwest and above Havre de Grace. As Birch's description suggests, the estate's lands extended from a substantial height to the shore of the Chesapeake to the south of the town. On Mount Pleasant, see Christopher Weeks, *An Architectural History of Harford County, Maryland* (Baltimore: Johns Hopkins University Press, 1996), 76–77.

55. Birch, "Life," 2: 13–14.

56. See Mona L. Dearborn, "Guy Atkinson and the Itinerant Artists of Fairfax Street, Alexandria," *Journal of Early Southern Decorative Arts* 22, no. 1 (1996): 1–41.

57. Birch's account of visits to Arlington and Woodlawn can be found in "Life," 2: 17–18.

58. Arlington House is now also known as the Robert E. Lee Memorial and located in Arlington National Cemetery. In accordance with conventional practice, the wings were built first. The central portion of the house was not completed until the mid-nineteenth century. On the construction of Arlington, see Murray Nelligan, "The Building of Arlington House," *Journal of the Society of American Historians* 10, no. 2 (1951): 11–15.

59. On Woodlawn, which was designed by architect William Thornton, see Carole McCabe, "Woodlawn Plantation," *Early American Life* 19, no. 1 (1988): 50–55.

60. Birch, "Life," 2: 12.

61. See Margaret Law Callcott, *Mistress of Riversdale: The Plantation Letters of Rosalie Stier Calvert* (Baltimore: Johns Hopkins University Press, 1991). For a discussion of Latrobe's designs for the house, see Jeffrey A. Cohen and Charles E. Brownell, *The Architectural Drawings of Benjamin Henry Latrobe* (New Haven: Published for the Maryland Historical Society and The American Philosophical Society by Yale University Press, 1994), 1: 291–295. See also Callcott, 28–29.

62. Henri J. Stier to Rosalie Stier Calvert, August 26, 1803, Henri J. Stier Papers, Maryland Historical Society, transcribed by Callcott, Landscape Chronology File, Riversdale Museum, Riverdale, Maryland; Callcott, *Mistress of Riversdale*, 53–54.

63. Callcott, *Mistress of Riversdale*, 134, 148.

64. See Callcott, *Mistress of Riversdale*, 180–181.

65. Birch, "Life," 2: 14–15.

66. Birch, "Life," 1: 48.

67. Despite the lack of support for the work, Birch apparently issued two editions of the book. According to collector Martin P. Snyder, the second appeared in 1827 or 1828. Snyder recorded that "the only copy of this edition yet found is in private hands. There must have been very few issued." Snyder, "William Birch: His

'Country Seats of the United States,'" *Pennsylvania Magazine of History and Biography* 83 (July 1957): 241n. No other copy of this later edition has come to light subsequently.

68. Fowble, *Two Centuries of Prints in America*, 74.

69. For a detailed and lucid discussion of Dickinson's revolutionary politics, see Jane E. Calvert, "Liberty Without Tumult: Understanding the Politics of John Dickinson," *Pennsylvania Magazine of History and Biography* 131, no. 3 (July 2007): 233–262.

70. On this subject, see Cooperman, "Belfield, Springland, and Early American Picturesque," 118–121; and Karol Ann Peard Lawson, "Charles Willson Peale's *John Dickinson*: An American Landscape as Political Allegory," *Proceedings of the American Philosophical Society* 136 (1992): 455–486.

71. The view is the frontispiece to the issue, the poem appears on page 607, with the direction to the reader to "see the elegant engraving prefixed to this number."

72. Gray's Inn, located on the western shore of the Schuylkill, was a popular spot of public refreshment in the early republican period and featured a well-known garden as part of its grounds.

73. Harris, *Artist in American Society*, 28–53.

74. For an extended discussion on this topic, see Laura Rigal, *The American Manufactory: Art, Labor, and the World of Things in the Early Republic* (Princeton: Princeton University Press, 1998).

75. Birch, "Life," 2: 23–24.

76. Published in the magazine *Port Folio* 3 (1807): 278–282.

77. See Cooperman, "William Russell Birch," chapter 5.

78. May 1791, description, 241, plate 240.

79. See Andrews, *Search for the Picturesque*, 24–38.

80. Karol Ann Peard Lawson, "An Inexhaustible Abundance: The National Landscape Depicted in American Magazines, 1780–1820," *Journal of the Early Republic* 12 (1992): 307. This interchangeability probably has its roots in the practice of extra-illustration in Britain in the eighteenth century; specifically, a volume on British history could be extra-illustrated with either portraits of important figures or images of specific places.

81. On this emblematic mode of landscape depiction and understanding, see Cooperman, "Belfield, Springland, and the Early American Picturesque."

82. Another, better-known example of such an improvement was Philadelphia's Fairmount Waterworks, which were seen at the time of their construction in the early nineteenth century as a great ornament to the Schuylkill. On the Waterworks, see Jane Mork Gibson, "The Fairmount Waterworks," *Philadelphia Museum of Art Bulletin* 84, nos. 360, 361 (Summer 1988).

83. Cornelius Stafford, *Philadelphia Directory for 1804* (Philadelphia: Printed for the editor by William Woodward, 1804), 3.

84. Jefferson's paean to the Virginia yeoman farmer ("those who labour in the earth are the chosen people of God, if ever he had a chosen people") can be found in his *Notes on the State of Virginia*, ed. William Peden (reprint, New York: W. W. Norton, 1972), 164–165.

85. For a concise and lucid discussion of these concepts, and some of the ancient writing on the subject of country life, see James S. Ackerman, *The Villa: Form and Ideology of Country Houses* (Princeton: Princeton University Press, 1990), 35–41.

86. See Ackerman, *The Villa*, 9–34.

87. See Lynn Dakins Hastings, *Guidebook to Hampton National Historic Site* (Towson, Md.: Historic Hampton, 1986), 3–21.

88. On Smith, see John S. Pancake, *Samuel Smith and the Politics of Business* (Montgomery: University of Alabama Press, 1972), and Frank A. Cassell, *Merchant Congressman in the Young Republic: Samuel Smith of Maryland, 1752–1839* (Madison: University of Wisconsin Press, 1971). On the subject of earlier illicit trade by Philadelphians, see Theodore Thayer, "Town into City," in Weigley, ed., *Philadelphia*, 73.

89. See Daniel M. Friedenberg, "The Strange Case of Robert Morris," in *Life, Liberty and the Pursuit of Land: The Plunder of Early America* (Buffalo, N.Y.: Prometheus Books, 1992), 338–347. On Cramond's connection to Morris, see Correspondence and business papers of Philips, Cramond and Co., Claude W. Unger Collection; and Philips, Cramond and Co. Papers, Society Collection, Historical Society of Pennsylvania, Philadelphia.

90. Sedgeley was sold at a sheriff's sale to Samuel Mifflin on September 11, 1806. J. Cohen and O. Robbins, Sedgeley research notes, 1995, 3, courtesy Jeffrey A. Cohen, Philadelphia.

91. See Mary Black, *New York City's Gracie Mansion: A History of the Mayor's House* (New York: Published for the Gracie Mansion Conservancy by the J. M. Kaplan Fund, 1984), 46–48.

92. On van Braam, who added Hoockgeest to his name in later life, see Jean Gordon Lee, *Philadelphians and the China Trade, 1784–1844* (Philadelphia: Philadelphia Museum of Art, 1984), 81–91. For a detailed contemporary description of the house, see Julian Ursyn Neimcewicz, *Under Their Vine and Fig Tree*, ed. and trans. Metchie J. E. Budka (Elizabeth, N.J.: Grassman Publishing Company, 1965), 62–63.

The Country Seats of the United States

William Russell Birch

Plate 1. Title Page

The Capitol at Washington.

Designed and Published by W. Birch, Enamel Painter, Springland near Bristol, Pennsylv.a 1808.

Birch's characteristically oblique writing in this introduction to the *Country Seats* establishes several key themes of his book. His opening declares the important role of his subject in helping to create the new American culture, a claim at least partly borne out by the enduring significance of suburban life in the United States to the present. He also asserts that the professional practice of landscape design (the "fine arts") in creating a country house property for the nation's wealthy citizens will establish a leading example and thus help forge this new American civilization. The crucial role of American nature and its inherent variety (its "sportive"-ness) in creating a "Country Residence" is also championed. Birch thus warns his reader that his subject is the cultural landscape context of the country house as much as—if not more than—the architecture of the dwelling itself. His interest in and emphasis on "wild unregulated nature" was a relatively new and unusual idea in the United States in the period, although it was one that would become enormously popular later in the nineteenth century.

AMERICAN SEATS.

THE Fine Arts are, as to the American Nation at large, in their infancy; to promote them in propagating Taste with the habit of rural retirement, supported by the growing wealth of the Nation, will be to form the National character favourable to the civilization of this young country, and establish that respectability which will add to its strength.

The comforts and advantages of a Country Residence, after Domestic accommodations are consulted, consist more in the beauty of the situation, than in the massy magnitude of the edifice: the choice ornaments of Architecture are by no means intended to be disparaged, they are on the contrary, not simply desirable, but requisite. The man of taste will select his situation with skill, and add elegance and animation to the best choice. In the United States the face of nature is so variegated; Nature has been so sportive and the means so easy of acquiring positions fit to gratify the most refined and rural enjoyment, that labour and expenditure of Art is not so great as in Countries less favoured.

It would be impossible to do justice in a work, such as this is intended to be, without appropriating some plates to the sports of wild unregulated nature: the Woods, Lawns, broken Precipices and Crags: the curious and sublime of the Forest Trees: the Cataracts and Rivers: the blue Capt Mountains, and the deep, retired, and darksome Vallies.

Such scenes which decorate the grounds, and form the choicest Pictures of themselves, and which cannot be brought into the same Plate with the Villa, will be given separately, as highly necessary to form a full and correct idea of the American Country Residence.

Plate 2. Frontispiece. Springland, which is represented in both the frontispiece and the last plate of the set, was located near the mouth of Neshaminy Creek and the Delaware River to the north of Philadelphia in Bucks County, Pennsylvania. In 1798, it was purchased by William Birch, who had designed and at least in part implemented improvements there by the date of the publication of the *Country Seats*, despite having lost the property to creditors in 1805. Birch repurchased the property in 1813 and sold it in 1818 at a profit.* No part of Birch's work there survives.

* Martin P. Snyder, "William Birch: His 'Country Seats of the United States'," *Pennsylvania Magazine of History and Biography* 81 (July 1957): 230n, 234.

HOBOKEN,

IS seated upon a prominent rock on the North River ; and commands an extensive view, embracing New-York, Long Island, Staten Island, Governor's Island, and the Bay to the Narrows, and on the other hand, a perspective of North River.*

Plate 3. Hoboken, or Hoebuck, was built by inventor and Revolutionary War officer John Stevens (1749–1838).[†] In 1784, Stevens purchased the large estate, which had been confiscated from a loyalist, and which corresponded roughly to the city of Hoboken, New Jersey. The Stevens villa was built shortly after the land purchase. It stood on part of the campus of the Stevens Institute of Technology, founded by the family after the Civil War. Thus, Birch's view is toward the north, showing the Hudson River (known at the time by the name Birch gives it) at right, with the New Jersey Palisades in the background.

*The description included here and those that follow for each plate are transcriptions of Birch's text as it appears in his original publication, including his variant spellings and typographical errors. The letterpress descriptions originally were printed together over three pages and bound into the volume.
[†]On Stevens, see Archibald Douglas Turnbull, *John Stevens: An American Record* (New York: Century Co., 1928). The Stevens family papers, which are extensive, are preserved in the collection of the New Jersey Historical Society in Newark.

Hoboken *in New Jersey*, the Seat of Mr. John Stevens.

Drawn Engraved & Published by W.Birch. Springland near Bristol. Pennsylva.

HAMPTON,

Stands on a spherical rise of ground, from whose valley emerges a wide amphitheatre of elegant inland country.

Plate 4. The Hampton estate, located in Towson, Maryland, and now a National Historic Site, encompassed some 25,000 acres at the time Birch published the *Country Seats*. The house was built by "Captain" Charles Ridgely beginning in 1783; his initial purchase of acreage that would become part of the estate took place in 1745. Construction on the mansion continued until his death in 1790, when the property was inherited by his nephew Charles Carnan Ridgely (1760–1829).* Birch visited the estate in the first years of the nineteenth century and made drawings for landscape work there. Birch's view shows the north elevation of the main house.

* See Lynn Dakins Hastings, *Guidebook to Hampton National Historic Site* (Towson, Md.: Historic Hampton, 1986). As the military title in Birch's plate caption suggests, Charles Carnan Ridgely attained the rank of brigadier general in the Eleventh Maryland Brigade. Ridgely later served as governor of Maryland (1815–1817).

Hampton *the* Seat *of* Gen.ˡ Cha.ˢ Ridgley, *Maryland*.—

Drawn Engraved & Published by W. Birch Springland near Bristol Penns.ᵃ

LANDSDOWN,

Lies upon the bank of the Pastoral Schuylkill, a stream of peculiar beauty, deservedly the delight and boast of the shores it fertilizes. The house was built upon a handsome and correct plan by the former governor Penn.

Plate 5. Lansdowne (preferred spelling), formerly located on the Schuylkill River's west bank, was built by John Penn (1729–1795) soon after his appointment as colonial governor of Pennsylvania in 1773. Penn (a grandson of Pennsylvania's founder) and his wife, Anne, née Allen, occupied the property as a retreat from the turbulent events of the Revolution and its aftermath at various points until they left for England in 1788, returning in 1792. During their absence, William Bingham (1752–1804) and his wife, Anne (née Willing, 1764–1801), rented Lansdowne as their country house in the summers. The Binghams were among the wealthiest citizens of the new republic and central figures in the "Federalist Court" of George Washington's tenure in office in Philadelphia. They purchased the property in 1797 at a sheriff's sale after speculator James Greenleaf (married to Ann Penn's niece, who had inherited the estate) had to liquidate assets to meet his creditors' demands. The Binghams did not occupy it for long, since both died in the first years of the nineteenth century (as Birch's plate text suggests). The house was largely destroyed by fire in the middle of the nineteenth century and was demolished completely before the Centennial.*

*On the Penns during their ownership of Lansdowne, see Lorett Treese, *The Storm Gathering: The Penn Family and the American Revolution* (University Park: Pennsylvania State University Press, 1992), chaps. 15–17; on the Binghams, see Margaret L. Brown, "Mr. and Mrs. William Bingham of Philadelphia," *Pennsylvania Magazine of History and Biography* 61 (July 1937): 286–324; and on Lansdowne, see Roger W. Moss, *The American Country House* (New York: Henry Holt, 1990), 81–85.

Landsdown *the Seat of the late* W.m Bingham Esq.r *Pennsylvania.*

Drawn Engraved & Published by W. Birch Springland near Bristol Pennsylv.a

ECHO,

An elegant situation on the bank of the Schuylkill, near the suburbs of the city: rich in every wild luxury which nature can afford to the plastic hand of art. The house is of no note, and its scite not well chosen. It derives its name from the reverberations given from the opposite shore—particularly by a rock memorable for having been in the revolution the place of encampment for the British, while Gen. Washington and his army were on this spot.

Plate 6. Little is known either about this property or the owner, whose name was probably spelled "Beveridge." A drawing by J. P. Malcom labeled with this name and showing a small, cubic villa is the only known image of the house.* "Beveridge" also appears on the western shore of the river just above the upper ferry on the 1796 Peter C. Varlé plan of Philadelphia and its surroundings, indicating the site of the property,† and David Beveridge, an insurance broker (the only person listed with this surname), appears in contemporary Philadelphia directories. Birch displayed the watercolor on which this print was based at Springland in his art collection; it was the only work of his included in the didactic exhibition there. A watercolor of the subject, presumably the same painting, survives in the collection of the Corcoran Museum of Art, Washington, D.C.

* Martin Snyder, *City of Independence* (New York: Praeger, 1975), figure 97.
† Snyder, *City of Independence*, 198–201.

The Sun reflecting on the Dew, a Garden scene.
Echo, Pennsyl^a. a place belonging to M^r. D. Bavarage.

Drawn Engraved & Published by W. Birch Springland near Bristol Pennsylvania.

MOUNT VERNON,

This hallowed mansion is founded upon a rocky eminence, a dignified height on the Potomac. During the French war, Admiral Vernon, who commanded the British fleet on this station, frequently made visits to his friend the father of Gen. W. and thence is derived its name. The additions of a piazza to the water front, and of a drawing room, are proofs of the legitimacy of the General's taste. It is now the residence of Judge Washington.

Plate 7. Birch visited Mount Vernon about 1803, as well as Woodlawn and Arlington House, the nearby properties of Washington's Custis relatives.

Mount Vernon, *Virginia*, the Seat of the late Genl G. Washington.

Drawn Engraved & Published by W. Birch Springland near Bristol Pennsylv.^a

FOUNTAIN GREEN,

On the Schuylkill, highly favored by nature, and capable of vast improvement. Upon the half ascent of the bank from the river, the new canal will pass the house and if ever finished, will become a great ornament to the place.

Plate 8. At the time of Birch's print, Fountain Green, long since demolished, was owned by Philadelphia merchant Samuel Meeker, who had purchased it from the Mifflin family at the turn of the nineteenth century. Merchant Jonathan Mifflin (1753–1840) sold the property at auction in July 1799, after the death of his father, John Mifflin (1720–1798), also a merchant. The newspaper advertisements for the sale give a concise idea of the features of the sorts of properties Birch depicted. Fountain Green included 25 acres of land "divided into lots" and a "good two-story stone dwelling house, with two rooms on the first floor, three on the second, and two ceiled garrets; two stone wings, one occupied as a kitchen, the other as a lodging room; a good stone barn, with stable room for eight horses; a frame cow stable, having stalls for seven cows, and hay-loft above; a most excellent spring house, with suitable accommodations for a tenant, or overseer; a plunging bath, covered with a neat frame building, used as a wash house, two good bearing orchards of the best kinds of grafted fruit; highly cultivated [vegetable] gardens, and a variety of different kinds of fruit trees, and grape vines."*

One of principal motives behind the construction of the Schuylkill canal was to enable coal to be transported more readily from upriver. The portion of the canal shown in Birch's view does not survive.

* On the Mifflins: see Jean Gordon Lee, *Philadelphians and the China Trade, 1784–1844* (Philadelphia: Philadelphia Museum of Art, 1984), 109. The sale of the property in 1799 was advertised in Philadelphia newspapers throughout the spring of that year, apparently without finding a buyer. The July 11 auction was also announced in several newspapers, including Claypoole's *American Daily Advertiser* for July 9, 1799.

Fountain Green *Pennsylv.ᵃ the Seat of* Mr. S. Meeker.

Drawn Engraved & Published by W. Birch Springland near Bristol Pennsylvania.

SOLITUDE.

Here a pleasing solitude at once speaks the propriety of its title. Upon further research the solitary rocks, and the waters of the Schuylkill add sublimity to quietness. The house is built with great taste for a bachelor, by the former Governor John Penn, since the revolution.

Plate 9. The house survives today on the grounds of the Philadelphia Zoo, although the kitchen (seen to the left of the house in Birch's view) does not. The Solitude was built by John Penn (1760–1834), the younger first cousin of the Lansdowne builder of the same name. The younger Penn, often styled either "the poet" for his published writing or "of Stoke" for the location of his residence in Buckinghamshire, first came to Philadelphia in the fall of 1783 in the attempt to secure the family's proprietary holdings after the Revolution. Soon after his arrival, Penn purchased 15 acres on the Schuylkill and built the casino depicted here in 1784–1785. He recorded that "I had then a notion of the possibility of settling in the country, tho not much of the probability."* After returning to England in 1788, Penn never again saw the Solitude, and the property was rented through the remainder of the eighteenth century, as Birch documents in his autobiography.†

* John Penn Commonplace Book, Collection the Historical Society of Pennsylvania, Philadelphia, 34v.

† On John Penn and his efforts to secure the family's interests in Pennsylvania: see Treese, *The Storm Gathering*, chap. 18; on the Solitude, see, for example, Roger W. Moss, *Historic Houses of Philadelphia* (Philadelphia: University of Pennsylvania Press, 1998), 66–71. Birch also painted a similar view in oil which is preserved in the collection of the Winterthur Museum, Delaware.

Solitude in Pensylv.ª belonging to Mr. Penn.

Drawn Engraved & Published by W. Birch Springland near Bristol Pensylv.ª

DEVON,

An airy and pleasant situation on the Pennsylvania shore of the Delaware, fourteen miles from Philadelphia. The house was built by Mr. Jos. Anthony.

Plate 10. Both the builder of Devon, prominent merchant Joseph Anthony (painter Gilbert Stuart's uncle), and his son, the silversmith Joseph Anthony, Jr., subscribed to Birch's *City of Philadelphia*. The elder Anthony sold the property at auction in April 1804, advertising the 57¾-acre "Country Seat and Farm" in Philadelphia newspapers as being "at a convenient distance and in sight of the post-road to New York, commanding a view of 15 miles." The "mansion house" corresponds closely to Birch's depiction: "50 feet square, with two pavilions 25 feet square with covered passage to each." The farm included "a large garden well stocked with the finest grafted peaches, pears, plumbs [sic], nectarines, apricots &c. &c. and very extensive raspberry, strawberry and asparagus beds" as well as a "large stone barn 45 feet square with stalls for 14 horses, a carriage house that will contain 6 carriages, cow house, poultry house, ice house, &c. &c. and a very neat and convenient tenant house." The advertisement concluded by asserting that "the whole of the buildings are built of the best materials, and in the most substantial manner, and in the stile [sic] of elegance far superior to any other House on the banks of the Delaware."* At the time of Birch's view, Devon was owned by Alexander J. Dallas (1759–1817), who retained it until his death. The house shown here was destroyed by fire in the mid-nineteenth century.†

* "For Sale, a Handsome Country Seat and Farm," *Poulson's American Daily Advertiser*, February 17, 1804.

† In 1893, the Reverend Samuel F. Hotchkin noted in connection with the property and that adjacent, known as Chelwood, that "the houses were built within the last twenty-five years to replace others which were destroyed by fire." Hotchkin, *The Bristol Pike* (Philadelphia: George W. Jacobs & Co., 1893), 291.

Devon *in Pennsylv.a* the Seat of M.r Dallas.

Painted by T. Birch, Engraved & Published by W. Birch Springland near Bristol Pennsylvania.

MOUNT SIDNEY,

Derives its honorable name from the patriot Algernon, who died in the reign of Charles II. a martyr to liberty. Its sylvan scene mingle with the romantic wilds of Sedgely.

Plate 11. John Barker (d. 1818) was a popular Philadelphia politician, serving (separately) as sheriff and as mayor, although his original occupation was as a tailor. He was commissioned as a lieutenant in the Pennsylvania militia in 1777 and became brigadier general of the militia after the war. Birch painted enamels of both Barker and his wife, and in 1820 he sold the portrait of the general in a raffle, a common means of selling artwork in the period.* Barker purchased Mount Sidney in 1805 and owned it until 1813.†

Mount Sidney was named, as Birch indicates, for the Republican political writer Algernon Sidney (1623–1683). Sidney, although an aristocrat, fought on the side of Cromwell in the Civil War, and was executed for his purported involvement with the Rye House plot to assassinate Charles II. Sidney was taken up as a martyr by the Whigs, and thus by many Americans.‡ The house, built before the turn of the nineteenth century, stood on a three-acre plot of land to the east and inland of Sedgeley (plate 15), and thus, lacking the unobstructed water view, presumably reflected the somewhat poorer economic circumstances of its owner relative to his immediate Schuylkill merchant neighbors. Mount Sidney had been demolished by the mid-nineteenth century.§ This is the only known view of it.

* On Barker, see Henry Simpson, *The Lives of Eminent Philadelphians, Now Deceased* (Philadelphia: William Brotherhead, 1859), 25–26. The enamels survive in the collection of the Walters Art Museum, Baltimore, Maryland. Birch's manuscript "Book of Profits" (private collection) records the raffle.

† J. Cohen and O. Robbins, Sedgeley research notes, 1995, 3, courtesy Jeffrey A. Cohen, Philadelphia.

‡ Jonathan Scott, "Sidney, Algernon (1623–1683)," *Oxford Dictionary of National Biography*, Oxford University Press, September 2004; online edition, October 2007 (http://www.oxforddnb.com/view/article/25519, accessed November 18, 2007).

§ The location and size of the property is recorded in several period maps, including the R. Howell 1799 survey of the Hills (copied by J. Hill, 1799, copied by R. Campbell, 1827), Fairmount Park Commission Archives, Philadelphia. The house ceases to appear on maps of Fairmount Park before the Civil War.

Mount Sidney, the Seat of Genl. John Barker, Pennsylva.

Drawn, Engraved & Published by W. Birch, Springland, near Bristol, Pensylvania.

THE SEAT OF Mʀ. DUPLANTIER,

Exhibits a style of building familiar to the West Indies, and well adapted to the warm climate of our newly acquired territory. The situation is verdant, and throughout the year, the air is fragrant with the perfume of orange groves. In the distance is descried the port and shipping of New Orleans.

Plate 12. The Delord-Sarpy mansion, built about 1765, was purchased in 1807 by Armand Duplantier (1753–1827), a former aide-de-camp of Lafayette, as part of property he expected to develop on speculation in what is now the New Orleans Garden District.* As Birch's note opposite indicates, for a time the house was the headquarters of General James Wilkinson (1757–1825), who was named governor of Louisiana Territory in 1805. The house was demolished in the late nineteenth century.

The drawing from which this print was made was created by Birch's son George (b. 1783), who served under Wilkinson and continued in the military for the rest of his career.

* S. Frederick Starr, *Southern Comfort: The Garden District of New Orleans* (New York: Princeton Architectural Press, 2005), 16; Samuel Wilson, Jr., and Bernard Lemann, *New Orleans Architecture* 1 (New Orleans: Friends of the Cabildo and Pelican Publishing, 1971).

Drawn by G. Birch, Cornet of Light Dragoons, U.S. Army.

The Seat of Mr. Duplantier near New Orleans, & lately occupied as Head Quarters, by Genl. J. Wilkinson.

Engraved & Published by W. Birch Springland near Bristol Pennsylva.

MONTIBELLO,

Handsomely seated amid the woods, a few miles from Baltimore, and commanding a prospect of the Chesapeake and Baltimore Bays. The house was built by Gen. S. Smith, from a plan and elevation by Mr. W. Birch, the proprietor of this work, and is generally approved.

Plate 13. Birch's responsibility for the design of Montebello (preferred spelling) is recorded by his statement above and by the plan preserved in the collection of the Baltimore Museum of Art (see figure 13). Construction is reported to have begun on the house in 1799.* This date suggests that Birch supplied the owner, Samuel Smith (1752–1839), with a plan while Smith was in Philadelphia as a U.S. Representative, since Birch probably did not travel south to Baltimore until after the turn of the nineteenth century (Smith also later served as a U.S. Senator). The Montebello estate encompassed some 500 acres, with "grounds finely laid out in the English style."† The house itself was demolished in 1909, but its appearance is recorded in several photographs and publications.‡

* J. Gilman Paul, "Montebello, Home of General Samuel Smith," *Maryland Historical Magazine* 42, no. 4 (December 1947): 255.
† *Baltimore: Past and Present* (Baltimore: Richardson and Bennett, 1871), 465.
‡ In addition to Paul's article, see Lawrence Hall Fowler, "Montebello, Maryland," *Architectural Review* 16 (1909): 145–149. Several late nineteenth- and early twentieth-century photographs of the house survive in the collection of the Maryland Historical Society.

Montibello *the Seat of* Gen.l S. Smith *Maryland*.

Drawn Engraved & Published by W. Birch Springland near Bristol Pennsylv.a

WOODLANDS.

This noble demesne has long been the pride of Pennsylvania. The beauties of nature and rarities of art, not more than the hospitality of the owner, attract to it many visitors. It is charmingly situated on the winding Schuylkill, and commands one of the most superb water scenes that can be imagined. The ground is laid out in good taste. There are here a hot house and green house containing a collection in the horticultural department, unequalled perhaps in the United States. Paintings &c. of the first master embellish the interior of the house, and do credit to Mr. Wm. Hamilton, as a man of refined taste.... It is about a mile from the city of Philadelphia.

Plate 14. William Hamilton's (1745–1813) architectural and landscape accomplishments at the Woodlands in the late 1780s were noticed by many in addition to Birch, including Thomas Jefferson.[*] In his autobiography, Birch also specifically noted Hamilton's approval of Springland.[†] Hamilton inherited the Woodlands and a considerable fortune in 1747 when he was still a small child, and the greatest developments he made there took place in the late 1780s after he returned to Philadelphia from a journey to England in 1784–1786. He came back with plans from an unidentified architect for the house and inspiration for planting his landscape garden.[‡] An accomplished botanical collector and propagator (as Birch indicates), Hamilton substantially rebuilt and added to the 1740s house in 1788–89 and developed what was among the most publicly admired gardens in the American early republic.[§] The house became the company offices for a rural cemetery (that is, landscaped rather than the churchyard type) in 1843, and still serves as such.

[*] Jefferson described the Woodlands as "the only rival I have known in America to what may be seen in England." Jefferson to Hamilton, July 1806, in Edwin M. Betts, ed., *Thomas Jefferson's Garden Book, 1766–1824* (Philadelphia: American Philosophical Society, 1944), 322–324.

[†] Birch, "Life," 3:3.

[‡] A professional architect's responsibility for the additions and alterations to the Woodlands was first discussed in scholarly publication by Richard Betts, "The Woodlands," *Winterthur Portfolio* 14, no. 3 (1979): 14–15. John Plaw, best known for his pattern book publications, and Henry Ashley Keeble, who designed new entrance gates for William Bingham at Lansdowne, have been posited as candidates for the designer. Moss, *Historic Houses*, 78.

[§] For a detailed account of Hamilton's landscape activities, see Timothy Preston Long, "The Woodlands: A 'Matchless Place,'" master's thesis, Historic Preservation program, University of Pennsylvania, 1991. On the Woodlands and its cultural role, see James A. Jacobs, "William Hamilton and the Woodlands: A Construction of Refinement in Philadelphia," *Pennsylvania Magazine of History and Biography* 103, no. 2 (2006): 181–209.

Woodlands *the Seat of* Mr. Wm. Hamilton *Pennsylv.a*

Drawn, Engraved & Published by W. Birch, Springland near Bristol, Pennsylvan.a

SEDGELY.

This beautiful gothic structure, which so happily graces the luxuriant banks of Schuylkill, is in the neighbourhood of Landsdown, which is seen in the distance on the opposite side of the river, whose gentle stream courses lowly and humble, amidst romantic woods, gently descending lawns and caverned rocks. The house was erected by Mr. Crammond, from a design by that able architect, Mr. J. H. Latrobe.*

Plate 15. Sedgeley (preferred spelling) was one of the first Gothic Revival houses to be built in the United States, and may have influenced the form of Birch's own house at Springland.† Built in 1799–1800 for merchant William Cramond from designs by the important architect Benjamin Henry Latrobe (1764–1820), the main house survived until 1857. Cramond named the property, which he owned for less than a decade, for the country house of his British business associate Thomas Philips.‡

The tenant house, commonly called the Guard House, survives today as the offices of the Fairmount Park Historic Preservation Trust.

* Birch mistook the architect's first initial.

† The current location of Birch's view of the buildings at Springland, which shows lancet-arch details and window labels on both structures depicted, is unknown. The watercolor was sold at auction in 1980. See Emily T. Cooperman, "Belfield, Springland and Early American Picturesque: The Artist's Garden in the American Early Republic," *Studies in the History of Gardens & Designed Landscapes* 26, no. 2 (2006): 127. Sedgeley and Latrobe's design and drawings are thoroughly documented by Jeffrey A. Cohen and Charles E. Brownell, *The Architectural Drawings of Benjamin Henry Latrobe* (New Haven: Published for the Maryland Historical Society and The American Philosophical Society by Yale University Press, 1994), 1: 254–259.

‡ See Thomas Philips & Co. to William Cramond, July 14, 1790, Philips, Cramond & Co. Papers, Historical Society of Pennsylvania, Philadelphia.

Sedgley, the Seat of Mr. Wm. Crammond Pennsylva.

Drawn Engraved & Published by W. Birch Springland near Bristol Pennsylvania.

BELMONT.

It is impossible for the artist, who has fixed his attention upon the various beauties of Schuylkill, to leave the study of its charms. Here you pass from the wild romantic scene; the rugged stone with wood and water bound to expand the sight from this high lifted lawn, to view in open space the world below, the riches of the richest state; the big metropolis in the woods, the chequered country with her merchants' seats; the bustle of agriculture, and the verdant banks of the fluid mirror that reflects the sky; and further on to view Mount Holly mingled with the air in Jersey. The whole a soft and visionary scene.

Plate 16. The villa at Belmont, the property of the Peters family, was built in the 1740s, and by the 1760s had an extensive ornamental garden that would have been very old-fashioned in Birch's terms.* At the time of Birch's view, the property was owned by Richard Peters (1743–1828), judge for the United States District Court of Pennsylvania. Peters was a leader among Philadelphia's elite progressive farmers and a member of the Philadelphia Society for Promoting Agriculture. The house retains remarkable eighteenth-century decorative plasterwork. Although a story was added to the building in the mid-nineteenth century, its original eighteenth-century appearance was recorded by Joshua Rawley Watson in 1816.†

Belmont is open to the public as one of the historic houses in Fairmount Park. Birch later painted a similar view in oil, now in the collection of the Winterthur Museum, Delaware.

* See George Vaux, ed., "Extracts from the Diary of Hannah Callender," *Pennsylvania Magazine of History and Biography* 12 (1888): 454–455.

† Kathleen A. Foster, ed., *Captain Watson's Travels in America: The Sketchbooks and Diary of Joshua Rawley Watson, 1771–1818* (Philadelphia: University of Pennsylvania Press, 1997), pl. 25. The most extensive documentation of Belmont can be found in Martin Jay Rosenblum, R.A. and Associates, "Belmont Mansion Historic Structures Report" (January 1992), Fairmount Park Commission Archives. See also Moss, *Historic Houses*, 62–64.

View from Belmont Pennsyl.a the Seat of Judge Peters.

Drawn Engraved & Published by W. Birch Springland near Bristol Pennsyl.a

YORK ISLAND.

This view is taken from the piazza of the seat of General Stevens on Long Island, near that extraordinary channel called Hell-gate, on the East river, or sound. The view was taken in the morning at the rising of the sun, when a glow of light from the arch of Heaven, exhibited to the view almost innumerable seats, spread over an extensive country which glittered as the sun arose, like so many stars in the firmament, upon the face of this beautifully variegated Island. The scene extending across the North river to the Jersey shore.

Plate 17. Birch's view of the upper east side of Manhattan Island records the villa district of Hell Gate, as well as its landscape surroundings in the early nineteenth century. The area was named, as Birch suggests, for the view of the East River. Of the properties shown here, only Archibald Gracie's mansion, highlighted left of center, survives. The house, which has served as the official residence of the Mayor of New York, is now located in Carl Schurz Park.*

* On Gracie Mansion and its neighbors, see Mary Black, *New York City's Gracie Mansion: A History of the Mayor's House* (New York: published for the Gracie Mansion Conservancy by the J. M. Kaplan Fund, 1984), and Ellen Stern, *Gracie Mansion: A Celebration of New York City's Mayoral Residence* (New York: Rizzoli, 2005).

York – Island, with a View of the Seats of Mr. A. Gracie, Mr. Church &c.

Drawn, Engraved & Published by W. Birch, Springland, near Bristol, Penns.a

MENDENHALL FERRY.

This beautiful spot close upon the falls of Schuylkill, and central to the neighbouring seats of Philadelphia, is one of nature's choicest retreats. Mr. Mendenhall, to accommodate the citizens, has opened his house for public entertainment. The two seats on the bank, are those of Mr. Joseph Sims, and the justly celebrated Dr. Physick, the latter is called very appropriately Fairy Hill.

Plate 18. In Birch's view of part of the northern end of Philadelphia's Schuylkill River villa district below the falls shows Mendenhall's Prospect Lodge, which stood on the west bank of the river, and two properties located in what is now the central and northern sections of Laurel Hill Cemetery.* Merchant Joseph Sims's the Laurels is seen at left, and Fairy Hill, owned by another merchant, George Pepper (1779–1846), is shown at far right.† None of these buildings survives.

* See Aaron V. Wunsch, "Laurel Hill Cemetery," HABS No. PA–51–PHILA 100, Historic American Building Survey (HALS), National Park Service, U.S. Department of the Interior, 1999," Data pp. 12, 68 for dates of acquisition of these properties for the cemetery.

† It is not clear why Birch ascribed the ownership of Fairy Hill to Dr. Philip Syng Physick; perhaps Physick rented it when Birch visited the area.

Mendenhall Ferry, Schuylkill, Pennsylvania.

Drawn Engraved & Published by W. Birch Springland near Bristol Pennsylv.ª

CHINA RETREAT.

An airy and pleasant situation on the Delaware, 17 miles from Philadelphia. The house was built by Mr. Van Braam, late ambassador from Holland to China. It was here he prepared for the press his account of that embassy together with the manners and characters of the Chinese, and which was published at a great expense in London. Now the summer residence of the family of Mr. Manigaull, of S. Carolina.

Plate 19. Utrecht native and China trade merchant Andreas Everardus van Braam Houckgeest (1739–1801) and his family arrived in Charleston, South Carolina, in 1783. He traveled to China in the late 1780s and came to Philadelphia in 1796. That year, he purchased a property on the Delaware River, north of the city on the east side of the mouth of the Neshaminy Creek near Springland, and began construction on the house shown here. As Birch noted in his autobiography, van Braam ran into financial difficulties and, having been briefly put in prison, decided upon his release that he no longer wished to remain in the United States. He left in 1798.[*]

The house was featured in the 1802 *Traveller's Directory or a Pocket Companion ... from Philadelphia to New York and from Philadelphia to Washington*, where the authors described it as "a large elegant building, executed in the style of the East India dwellings."[†] A contemporary visitor's account described the house as "immense, surmounted with a cupola [see Figure 18] and decorated with golden serpents in the Chinese manner. Six tabourets of porcelain were arranged in a circle in the peristyle. The cellars are immense and the floor alone, made with great flags of stone, cost him 3,000 doll."[‡] In his autobiography, Birch wrote of the remarkable sight of van Braam on the river: "we [would] see him for a mile before, coming up with a rapid tide in his long boat, [with] his eight Chinese [servants] in white, trimming their oars to the water till he reached our bank giving me his first salute."[§]

At the time of the publication of the *Country Seats*, the property was owned by Gabriel Manigault, who rented it for a time to Joseph Bonaparte before the latter's purchase of Point Breeze.[**] China Retreat was demolished after 1939.

[*] Birch, "Life," 1: 44–45; Jean Gordon Lee, *Philadelphians and the China Trade, 1784–1844* (Philadelphia: Philadelphia Museum of Art, 1984), 81–82.

[†] S. S. Moore and T. W. Jones. *The Traveller's Directory or a Pocket Companion ... from Philadelphia to New York and from Philadelphia to Washington* (Philadelphia, 1802).

[‡] Julian Ursyn Neimcewicz, *Under Their Vine and Fig Tree*, ed. and trans. Metchie J. E. Budka (Elizabeth, N.J.: Grassman Publishing Company, 1965), 62–63.

[§] Birch, "Life," 1: 44.

[**] Harold Donaldson Eberlein and Cortlandt Van Dyke Hubbard, *Portrait of a Colonial City* (Philadelphia: J. B. Lippincott, 1939), 481.

China Retreat *Pennsyl*.^a *the Seat of* Mr Manigault.

Drawn, Engraved & Published by W. Birch Springland near Bristol Pennsylv.^a

SPRINGLAND.

This spot chosen by the artist for the exercise of his taste in retirement has peculiar beauties from nature. Art has added much to it, and the cottage is embellished with a small, but very fine collection of paintings by some of the first masters. This volume with his other works may be had at this place.

Plate 20. Birch's final engraving for the *Country Seats* brackets the work, along with the frontispiece, with his own property. The view here is from the central portion of his garden toward the east and the Neshaminy Creek.

View from the Elysian Bower, Springland Pennsylv.a the residence of Mr. W. Birch.

Drawn Engraved & Published by W. Birch Springland near Bristol Pennsyl.a

INDEX

Adam, Robert and James, 7, 11
Alexandria, Virginia, 18
Angus, William, 8
Annapolis, Maryland, 3, 13, 16, 17, 19
Anthony, Joseph, and Joseph, Jr., 60
Arlington House, Virginia, 18, 54, 37
Atkinson, Guy, 18

Baltimore, Maryland, 3, 12, 31
Barker, John, 62
Barlow, Joel, 23
Barralet, John James, 13
Barrow, Joseph Charles, 8, 11, 13; Figure 7
Bastille, Paris, fall of, 4
Belmont, Philadelphia, 1, 27, 30, 31, 32, 34, 35, 72; Plate 16
Beveridge, David, 52
Biddle, Nicholas, 34
Bingham, Anne, 12, 50
Bingham, William, 12, 33, 50
Birch, Albina (Mrs. Guy Atkinson), daughter, 18
Birch, Ann (Mrs. Thomas Chase), sister, 3
Birch, Anne (née Russell), mother, 3, 5
Birch, George, son, 64
Birch, Thomas, M.D., father, 3
Birch, Thomas, son, 13
Birch, William Russell; *City of Philadelphia in the State of Pennsylvania, North America, as it appeared in 1800*, 1, 2, 7, 12, 14, 15, 21, 25, 29, 30, 33, 60; Country house, Bucks County, Pennsylvania, *see* Springland; *Country Seats of the United States of North America*, 1, 2–4, 7, 10, 12, 13, 15, 21–29, 30–34, 38–81, *see also under individual sites*; *Délices de la Grande Bretagne*, 3, 6, 8–11, 14, 24–28, 30, 32, 36; Figures 1–4, 6–8; Early life and work in London, 3–7, 8–11; Enamel paintings by, 5, 6, 8, 12, 36, Figure 11; "Life" (autobiography), 4–10, 12–21, 24–25, 27, 31, 35, 36, 37, 68, 78; Landscape and architectural designs by, 15–16, 19–20, 45, 81; Figures 10, 11, 12, 13, Plates 2, 20; Travels through eastern states, 16–20
Birmingham, England, 3, 4, 5; Priestley riots, 4
Blenheim House, Oxfordshire, England, 8
Bonaparte, Joseph, 78
Braam, van, Andreas. *See* Houckgeest
Brown, Charles Brockden, 37
Brown, Lancelot "Capability," 11
Burke, Edmund, 9, 17, 18

Calvert, George and Rosalie (née Stier), 20
Canaletto, 6
Carroll, Charles (of Carrollton), 16
Castle Howard, Yorkshire, England, 32
Chase, Elizabeth and Ann, nieces, 16
Chase, Jeremiah T., 16–17
Chase, Samuel, 4, 16, 20
Chase, Thomas, 3, 16
Chauncey, Nathaniel, 6, 8–9, 10, 11, 36n
Chesapeake Bay, 18
China Retreat, Bucks County, Pennsylvania, 34, 78; Plate 19
Clymer, George, 25
Cole, Thomas, 2
Columbian Magazine, 22–23
Columbianum, 35–36
Columella, 23
Cooper, Richard, 11; Figure 8
Courbauld, Richard, 8
Cramond, William, 13, 33, 70
Custis, George Washington Parke, 18, 54

Dallas, Alexander J., 60
Delaware, State of, 16, 19, 30,

Delaware River, 13, 15, 23, 30, 34, 44, 60, 78
Delord-Sarpy Mansion, New Orleans, Louisiana, 1, 30, 64; Plate 12
Devon, Bucks County, Pennsylvania, 60; Plate 10
Dickinson, John, 21, 28; Figure 14
Downing, Andrew Jackson, 1, 2
Duncannon, Viscount (Frederic Ponsonby), 8
Duplantier, Armand, 64; Plate 12

Eaglesfield, Philadelphia, Pennsylvania, 13
East River, New York, 16, 31, 34, 74
Echo, Philadelphia, Pennsylvania, 12, 13, 27, 28, 30, 52; Plate 6
Enamel painting, 5–6, 7; Figure 5

Fairy Hill, Philadelphia, Pennsylvania, 31, 76; Plate 18
Farington, Joseph, 6, 8; Figure 6
Fort St. Davids Fishing Company, Philadelphia, Pennsylvania, 21
Fountain Green, Philadelphia, Pennsylvania, 28, 56; Plate 8

Gainsborough, Thomas, 8
Gilpin, William, 10
Gracie, Archibald, 16, 33, 74
Gracie Mansion, New York, New York, 16, 33, 35, 74
Gray's Ferry, Philadelphia, Pennsylvania, 22–23; Figure 15
Gray's Inn, Philadelphia, Pennsylvania, 38
Green Hill, North East, Maryland, 17
Greenleaf, James, 50
Groombridge, William, 13
Guillemard, John Lewis, 13

83

Hamilton, William, 24, 68
Hampton, Towson, Maryland, 1, 20, 32, 33, 34, 48; Plate 4
Hartley, Mrs. Mary, 8, 36
Havre de Grace, Maryland, 17
Hearne, Thomas, 8
Hell Gate villa district, New York City, 16, 31, 34, 74; Plate 17
Hills, the, Philadelphia, Pennsylvania, 33
Hoboken, New Jersey, 28, 32, 46; Plate 3
Horace, 23
Houckgeest, Andreas Everardus van Braam, 34, 38, 78
Hudson River, 16, 26, 31, 34, 44, 74
Hughes, Samuel, 17, 37

Jaudenes y Nebot, Josef de, 12
Jefferson, Thomas, 14, 17, 31, 33, 38, 68
Jefferys, Thomas, 3, 5, 6

Kenwood House, Hampstead Heath, London, 7, 11, 35; Figure 4
Knight, Richard Payne, 8, 10, 15

Lafayette, General (Marie-Joseph-Paul-Yves-Roch-Gilbert du Motier, Marquis de Lafayette), 13, 64
Lansdowne, Philadelphia, Pennsylvania, 12, 13, 27, 30–33, 50, 70; Plate 5
Latrobe, Benjamin Henry, 13, 20, 33, 37, 70
Laurel Hill Cemetery, Philadelphia, Pennsylvania, 76
Laurels, the, Philadelphia, Pennsylvania, 13, 31, 76; Plate 18
Letters from a Farmer in Pennsylvania, 21–22
Lewis, Lawrence and Eleanor (née Custis), 18, 26
Livingston, Henry, Figure 16

Lorrain, Claude, 10, 17, 36, 37
Loutherbourg, Philipp Jacob de, 8

Manigault, Gabriel, 78
Mansfield, first Earl of and Lord Chief Justice (William Murray), 7, 8, 11, 36
Maryland, State of, 16, 19, 27
Massachusetts Magazine, 28
Meeker, Samuel, 56
Mendenhall Ferry and Mendenhall Prospect Lodge, 13, 31, 76; Plate 18
Mercer, John, 16
Mifflin, John, 56
Mifflin, Jonathan, 56
Montebello, Baltimore, Maryland, 19, 33, 66; Figures 12 and 13; Plate 13
Morris, Gouverneur, 16
Morris, Robert, 33
Morrisiana, New York, 16
Mount Holly, New Jersey, 72
Mount Pleasant, Harford County, Maryland, 17, 37
Mount Sidney, Philadelphia, Pennsylvania, 31, 62; Plate 11
Mount Vernon, Virginia, 1, 13, 18, 24, 30, 32, 34, 54; Plate 7
Murray, William. *See* Mansfield

Neshaminy Creek, 26, 44, 78
New Orleans, Louisiana, 64
New York City, New York, 1, 12, 14, 16, 30–33, 46, 74; "York Island," *see* Hell Gate
New York Magazine, or Literary Repository, 26

Ouse Bridge at York, England, 6; Figure 6

Parkyns, George Isham, 8, 13–14, 21, 36
Peale, Charles Willson, 21, 22, 28, 35n; Figures 14, 15

Penn, John (governor) and Anne (née Allen), 50
Pepper, George, 76
Peters, Judge Richard, 72
Philadelphia, 7, 8, 12–14, 19, 31, 32; country seats and related sites, *see individual locations;* Fairmount Park, 2, 35, 70, 72; Fairmount Waterworks, 38; Pennsylvania Academy of the Fine Arts, 25
Philips, Thomas, 70
Physick, Philip Syng, 76
picturesque, 3, 8, 9–11, 13, 14, 17–18, 25, 26, 27, 36
Pliny the Younger, 23
Pocock, Nicholas, 8
Portsmouth, England, 8
Potomac River, 18–19
Priestley, Joseph, 4
Pouncy, Benjamin T., 8
Price, Uvedale, 10
Principio, Maryland (creek and forge), 3

Reinagle, Philip, 8
Repton, Humphry, 7, 35n
Reynolds, Sir Joshua, 3, 5, 6–7, 8, 11, 12, 25, 32, 35, 36n; Figure 1
Ridgeley, Charles Carnan, 20, 32, 48
Riversdale, Bladensburg, Maryland, 19–20
Roche, Frederic Franck de la, 13
Rodney, Caesar, 19
Rosa, Salvator, 10
Royal Academy of Arts, London, 3, 6, 8, 12,
Russell, Thomas, cousin, 16
Russell, Thomas, uncle, 3, 4, 5
Russell, William, cousin, 4–5

Saltram, Devon, England, 11; Figure 8
Scenographia Americana (1768), 21

Schuylkill River, 2, 8, 12–14, 21–23, 27, 28, 31–34, 50, 52, 56, 68, 72, 76
Shaw, Joshua (*Picturesque Views of American Scenery*), 1
Sedgeley, Philadelphia, Pennsylvania, 1, 13, 27, 31, 33, 38, 62, 70; Plate 16
Showell Green, near Birmingham, England, 4–5
Sidney, Algernon, 62
Sims, Joseph, 76
Smith, Judge Thomas, 13
Smith, General Samuel, 19, 33
Smith, Dr. William (provost of the University of Pennsylvania), 13
Solitude, the, Philadelphia, Pennsylvania, 13, 24, 31, 34, 58; Plate 9
Spicer, Henry, 5
Springland, Bucks County, Pennsylvania, 2, 13, 15–16, 27, 28, 32, 44, 68, 70, 78, 80; Figures 9–11; Plates 2 and 20

Stamp Act, opposition to, 21
Stevens, John, 32, 46
Stier, Henri-Joseph, 19
Strawberry Hill, Twickenham, England, 8, 11; Figure 7
Stuart, Gilbert, 12, 60
sublime, 9–11, 17–18, 26, 27
Susquehanna River, 17

Tiebout, Cornelius, Figure 16
Tilton, John, 19
Twickenham, near London, England, 11, 13. *See also* Strawberry Hill

Vernon, Admiral Edward, 54
Virgil, 23
Virginia, State of, 16, 18, 27

Walpole, Horace, 8, 11
Warwick, England, 3, 4; Figure 2
Washington, Augustine, 3

Washington, George, 3, 12, 18, 24, 28, 30, 34, 36, 50, 52, 54
Washington, Judge Bushrod, 54
Washington, Lawrence, 3, 54
Washington, Martha, 18
Washington, District of Columbia, 13, 14, 19, 30; Capitol Building, 30; Plate 1 (Title page); White House, 31
Watson, Joshua Rawley, 72
Wedgwood pottery, 6, 35
Wentworth Park, Yorkshire, England, 8
West, Benjamin, 3, 12
Whately, Thomas, 8
Wilkinson, General James, 64
Wilson, Richard, 3, 8
Woodlands, the, Philadelphia, Pennsylvania, 1, 13, 24, 27, 35, 68; Plate 14
Woodlawn, Virginia, 18–19, 37, 54

York, England, 6; Figure 6

Acknowledgments

Thanks are due first and foremost to the members of the Carson family—Wynne and Glenn Curry and Lea Sherk—whose copy of Birch's *Country Seats* is reproduced here. The quality of this copy is a testament to the remarkable collection of Birch's work assembled by Marian S. Carson. I would also like particularly to thank Lea Sherk for her generosity and for her fruitful collaboration on Birch, his career, and his work. I have been fortunate to have been assisted by many in addition to Mrs. Sherk over the course of several scholarly projects in recovering the details of Birch's life and work and the properties he depicted in the *Country Seats*. In connection with the preparation of this book, I would like particularly to thank Elizabeth Milroy for many stimulating conversations on the Schuylkill villas and Fairmount Park and both her and Jeffrey A. Cohen for generously sharing the fruits of their own scholarly labors. This book is dedicated to John, who has made it possible.